"Reading the Wind"

"Reading the Wind"

The Literature of the Vietnam War

An Interpretative Critique by Timothy J. Lomperis

With a Bibliographic Commentary by John Clark Pratt

Published for The Asia Society

Duke University Press

Durham 1987

Grateful acknowledgment is given for permission from the following authors to reprint their works in this volume:

W. D. Ehrhart, *To Those Who Have Gone Home Tired: New & Selected Poems* (New York: Thunder's Mouth Press, 1984), "Coming Home," p. 16, "Imagine," p. 19, "A Relative Thing," p. 17.

Bruce Weigl, *A Romance* (Pittsburgh: University of Pittsburgh Press, 1979), "Him, On a Bicycle," p. 30.

John Balaban, *After Our War* (Pittsburgh: University of Pittsburgh Press, 1974), excerpt from "Letter from a Bargirl"; *Ca Dao Vietnam* (Greensboro, N.C.: Unicorn Press), "Love Lament"; and for his translation of Ho Chi Minh's "On Reading the Anthology of the Ten Thousand Poets."

John Clark Pratt, for excerpts from *The Laotian Fragments* (New York: Avon Books, 1974) and *Vietnam Voices* (New York: Viking Penguin, 1984).

Contents

Foreword

In the eleven years since the withdrawal of the United States from Vietnam, Americans have agonized over the physical and psychological suffering caused by the war. They have questioned the policies and values that led the United States into Vietnam and sought to extract lessons from the experience. This effort to make sense of the Vietnam experience has prompted an outpouring of creative writing, including novels, short stories, poetry, personal accounts, and oral histories. Until recently this growing body of literature received relatively little attention, though it provides powerful and lasting perspectives on America's involvement in Vietnam. But gradually it is increasingly being viewed as an important development in contemporary American literature.

Recognizing that this new literature will shape how Americans view the Vietnam experience and our relations with Vietnam and Asia, The Asia Society sponsored a conference on "The Vietnam Experience in American Literature" on 7–9 May 1985. As a nonpartisan, educational organization, the Society believed that a program focusing on the literature written by Americans about the war would complement the Society's ongoing lectures and publications on Vietnam's culture and history. To the best of the Society's knowledge, the conference was the first gathering of many of the major authors of Vietnam War literature.

The purpose of the conference was to take stock of the Vietnam War literature and to assess its influence on present and future American perceptions of Vietnam and Asia. Major conference topics included the relationship of fact and fiction in the literature; the literature's reflection of American society and values during and after the war; images of Vietnam in the literature and the impact of these images on popular understanding of Vietnamese society and the war experience. The discussion among the nearly sixty writers, publishers, educators, and journalists who participated in the conference was articulate and thought-provoking. Two major themes emerged in the discussions: the relationship of politics to art and the impact of individual experiences on writings about the war. The conference showed that the politics of the war may be inseparable from the literature and that the literature offers a unique lens through which Americans can obtain a better understanding of themselves, their involvement in Vietnam, and their future in Asia.

This book contains two essays that were prepared as a result of the conference. John Clark Pratt's "Bibliographic Commentary" was commissioned in advance of the conference to provide a "road map" of the literature for the conference discussions. His selective review of approximately 140 of the more than 200 published works of fiction about the war provides both a critique of individual works and a method of ordering and orienting oneself to the overall body of literature.

Timothy J. Lomperis's "Interpretative Critique" evolved out of the Society's desire to provide a summary of the conference and a broad interpretation of the issues raised by the literature for American understanding of the war. Toward this end, Tim Lomperis has interwoven his own commentary with a report of the conference discussions. He sets out the conference's main issues, highlights key moments in the discussion by letting the authors speak through direct quotes, and sets the discussion in the larger context of history and values that surround all facets of the Vietnam experience.

In producing this conference and publication, The Asia Society was extraordinarily fortunate to have the advice and support of a number of individuals. In addition to early guidance from Lee Goerner, Lee Gray, Larry Lichty, and John Clark Pratt, we gratefully acknowledge the comments and suggestions of Peter Braestrup, William Ehrhardt, Larry Heinemann, Michael Stevens, and Jason Shinder. Our special thanks go as well to the more than sixty individuals who made time in their schedules to attend the two-day conference.

The Asia Society is particularly indebted to John Clark Pratt who was involved in the shaping of the project from the beginning and who gave so enthusiastically and generously of his time, particularly by fitting in another writing commitment in order to produce the essay for this book. Timothy J. Lomperis has the Society's deep appreciation and admiration for tackling a very difficult task while on research leave at Harvard, with most impressive results. Tim utilized his background as a political scientist and his personal interest in the literature to produce a truly integrative and thought-provoking essay. We are indebted to Tim for helping us to attain our objectives in this volume so clearly and for his enthusiasm, dedication, and skill.

Major financial support for the conference was generously provided by the Andrew J. Mellon Foundation through its overall support of The Asia Society's national public education program on contemporary Asian affairs, "America's Asian Agenda." The Asia Agenda program seeks to alert Americans to critical issues in Asian affairs and in U.S.-Asia relations, to illuminate the choices that public and private policymakers face, and to strengthen trans-Pacific dialogue on the issues. Our publisher, Duke University Press, was receptive to the idea and form of this volume, and we feel fortunate to have had their interest and flexibility in producing this book.

Finally, two members of the Society's staff were instrumental in the development of this publication. Eileen D. Chang ably supervised the majority of the book's production process. None of this effort would have been fruitful without the superb administrative assistance of Emily Collins.

Marshall M. Bouton, Director, Contemporary Affairs
Linda K. Kojabashian, Program Associate, Contemporary Affairs
David G. Timberman, Program Associate, Contemporary Affairs
September 1986

Acknowledgments

This book is both a commentary on a conference The Asia Society sponsored on the literature growing out of the divisive war in Vietnam and an interpretation of the place of this literature. It is perhaps fitting, since the war was as divisive in the United States as it was in Vietnam, that for my part of this work half of the book was written south of the Mason-Dixon linc at Duke University and the other half north of it at Harvard University's Center for International Affairs. During the period of this northern half, I received critical financial support from the Olin Foundation and the Earhart Foundation, for which I am deeply grateful. Since an evaluation of a literary genre is not a usual assignment for a political scientist, I have highly valued the encouragement I received from senior colleagues in my field, particularly from Ole Holsti and Allan Kornberg at Duke and from Sam Huntington and Sid Verba at Harvard. I am also very thankful—and relieved—to have the participation of John Clark Pratt in this venture. His superb bibliographic commentary gives this work a solid literary foundation.

This is not a usual conference report. It has, therefore, been subject to intense review. I have been encouraged by, and indebted to, the comments and suggestions of Peter Braestrup, Larry Heinemann, Bill Broyles, Frederick Downs, and John Clark Pratt, as well as those of the two anonymous reviewers for Duke University Press. The Asia Society is to be commended both for organizing a conference with such distinguished participants and for conceiving such an innovative plan for a "write-up." The lion's share of the credit here belongs to Linda Kojabashian, of the Society's Public

Affairs Department, who stuck with the project's manifold demands and my complications (a move and three family auto accidents) to the end. Now that we are at the "end," The Asia Society, as well as John Clark Pratt and I, are grateful to Duke University Press and Richard Rowson, its director, for having the foresight to publish this work.

What made the writing itself a sheer delight was the pleasant and competent clerical support I received, from Lib Franklin at Duke and from Janice Rand at Harvard who arranged for the help of Elizabeth Cox and Stacy Andersen. It tickles me that Elizabeth and Stacy are now avidly reading Vietnam War novels. The remaining roughage was heroically smoothed over by Bob Mirandon, my ever-patient, but always firm, copy editor at Duke University Press.

More generally, I could never have written this book with any sense of confidence without my own tour in Vietnam, and I owe the U.S. Army much for what was a very reluctant undertaking at the time. The most heartwarming harbinger of this project's worth was to watch the initial skepticism of my wife, Ana Maria, dissolve and turn to encouragement and helpful suggestions as the writing progressed. The cheerful little lives of our children Kristi and Scotty and the encouragement of my parents, I also have appreciated very much.

As a source of inspiration, I wish to pay tribute to all the novelists and poets of the Vietnam War. I have been entranced by their works. It is my hope that this slender volume will help spread their insights and call on others to add to them.

Naturally, this book is my responsibility, but it is the fault of everyone listed above who let me get away with it.

Interpretative Critique

"Reading the Wind"

---

by Timothy J. Lomperis

Introduction

The Shoals of Yin and Yang

Vietnam . . . [was] a two-lane highway, one for the Vietnamese and one for the Americans, with no intersections.—*Bernard and Marvin Kalb*, The Last Ambassador

Eleven years ago, on 30 April 1975, Saigon was the scene of jarring TV images that documented the end of a long war: of North Vietnamese tanks that slammed through the gates of the Presidential Palace and liberated the final citadel of South Vietnam's string of last, lost Confucians. Just the day before, American "Huey" helicopters had been shown plucking the final line of refugees from the rooftop of the American Embassy in "Operation Frequent Wind." Seeing the newsclips of this eleventh-hour evacuation, President Gerald Ford said to an aide, "It's over. Let's put it behind us."

Whatever else Americans have done with Vietnam, they have certainly not put it behind them. Everywhere in the Third World where the remotest prospect for American intervention in some local conflict looms, the ghost of Vietnam again and again casts its shadow. Today the "lessons" of Vietnam are invoked by both sides in the debate over the proper extent of American involvement in El Salvador and over the propriety of aid to the *contras* in Nicaragua. People draw their lessons from their memories, from that set of images which stays with them the longest. Some, with Ronald Reagan, remember Vietnam as a "noble crusade," while others relive with Daniel Ellsberg his nightmare of the war as a "heinous crime." Sorting out what happened in Vietnam, then, elusive as it continues to be, remains an important task if any coherence to these memories, and useful lessons from the "Vietnam experience," are ever to emerge.

In the literature, both in fiction and in nonfiction, this sorting continues, with the number of printed pages already voluminous. Despite the seeming finality of Hanoi's tanks rumbling into Saigon's urban jungles and flushing out flocks of fleeing American helicopters, the two-lane highway of the Vietnam War runs on "over here" in the minds, souls, and pens of Americans, still plagued by the dead war "over there," to a destination: who knows where? The Korean War ended in 1953, and that, more or less, was that. World War II ended in 1945, and it is still glorified. World War I lingered longer in the haunting disillusionment of Erich Maria Remarque's, *All Quiet on the Western Front,* or Ernest Hemingway's *A Farewell to Arms* and Maxwell Anderson and Laurence Stalling's play, *What Price Glory?* But all this blood of our grandparents' generation was washed away by the rush of our parents' generation scrambling to heed Franklin D. Roosevelt's call to erase America's "day of infamy." World War I is over; the Korean War is forgotten; World War II is an historical epic; but Vietnam festers on, eleven years after, as "the war that won't go away." The energy crisis, the national debt, the ticking international debt time bomb, Middle Eastern terrorism, and other distractions of our era have not been strong enough to extinguish our smoldering memories.

After an initial period of almost willful national amnesia, conferences have been convening in the last five years—in Washington, in Los Angeles, in New York—to "understand" America's "Vietnam trauma" or the "Second Indochina War." Most of these convening organizations have stuck to rather modest agendas, shunning the grandiose quest for lessons in favor of shedding light on more manageable subtopics. But as soon as the participants arrive, all they want to talk about is lessons. Whether grand ("What I want to point out is that everyone here is forgetting China") or small ("When I was in Chau Doc Province back in '63, the thing I noticed about the vc . . . "), it didn't matter. The "lessons" just erupt, overwhelming the tightly reasoned and erudite papers of the panelists and causing the dazed organizers to wonder where their conference went. The participants then leave, almost delightedly confused, eager to continue on with their quest to the next unsuspecting conference. Though this cycle may be somewhat overstated, the thirst for the lessons of Vietnam seems to be unquenchable. It is, after all, the only war America has not won, at least in recent memory.

The conference convened by the Asia Society in New York from 7 to

9 May 1985, was, in the words of Robert Oxnam, the society's president, "uniquely unique" in that it is the only one to look at the Vietnam experience through the literature on the war. In his welcoming remarks Oxnam, too, tried to resist the impulse for lessons. "One thing we don't want to do," he said, "is have yet another conference on the lessons of Vietnam." Still, in his charge to the participants after James Webb's keynote address, he told them to consider whether we can learn from history.

But the conference did more than weigh the lessons of Vietnam. In many ways it was a remarkable gathering. It was impressive in its substance. Conferees were treated to panels on "Combat Literature," "Fact and Fiction in the Literature," "Literature on the Veteran Experience," "The Impact on Those at Home," "Images of Asia and Asians in the Literature," and "The Role of Literature in Understanding the War." Threading through the panels were the themes that dominated the conference: an examination of the Vietnam War literature itself, the tension between fact and fiction, the Vietnamese as the great lost fact of the war, and future directions for, and responsibilities of, this literature.

To briefly elaborate, in sharing the observation that the literature so far has been derived from the first-hand experience of individual veterans, most conference participants concluded that it was time to expand the literature. Naturally, there was a wide divergence of views as to where, in particular, to go. On this question, a rather sharp debate ensued over whether the literature should still be based on some form of personal experience. These exchanges led to more philosophical ruminations over how factual a work of art had to be in service of the general cause of telling the truth. In telling this truth, since the American literature on the Vietnam War has thus far been based on the personal experience of American participants, it has had, as yet, little to say on the truth of the experiences of the Vietnamese themselves. How to overcome the special problems in bringing Vietnamese and Asian perspectives into the literature posed a central challenge to the entire conference. Finally, for a war whose place in American history is still mired in present controversy, settling on a future direction for its literature proved equally difficult. In a thought-provoking finale the conference participants were most comfortable with the term *fragments* and the offering of the *collage* as the most reflective literary form of this larger societal irresolution.

While this essay will largely be a perusal of these themes, I would be remiss if I did not at least point out that the conference at times edged into a replay of the Great Vietnam War Debate as well. It was an emotional presence that is not easily communicated to "outsiders." But this presence gave an important dynamic to the conference and, indeed, helped to sharpen people's articulation in the substantive areas.

The debate began with James Webb's keynote address, "Artistic Resolution, Societal Resolution," on the opening night of the conference. The effect of his speech was like a lightning bolt. To some, Webb's speech was a partisan and political defense of the Reagan administration's interpretation of the war as a "noble crusade." Quite obviously this was not an interpretation widely shared by the audience, at least to gauge by those who spoke. A few even voiced a sense of outrage that Webb's presenting of himself as a government spokesman represented an unwarranted intrusion of politics into a conference devoted to art and literature. If the purpose of a keynote speech is to be provocative and stimulating, Mr. Webb succeeded admirably.

The next morning's two panels on Literature on the War Experience ("Combat Literature" and "Fact and Fiction in the Literature") stuck fairly close to an analysis of the artistic problems writers of this literature have encountered, the more mundane difficulties in securing publishers, and the complicated question of whether a Vietnam War author owed his readers a good story or a rendition of the truth, and could he even attempt both? In the afternoon's two panels on Literature on the War's Impact on a Generation of Americans ("Literature on the Veteran Experience" and "The Impact on Those at Home"), the "debate" returned with a vengeance. Both panelists and speakers from the audience rose to denounce Webb's speech and the note of politicization it had injected into the conference. Some objected to the way that facts, in their view, had been twisted both proximately by Webb in his speech and by the government more generally throughout the war. In the course of these denunciations, some speakers outdid themselves (and James Webb) in their own political rhetoric.

This sentiment came to a head in Ron Kovic's speeches during the afternoon's second panel. They were a fairly explicit rejoinder, even a backlash, to Webb's speech, and had much the same galvanizing impact as Webb had earlier, though obviously from a different perspective. Ron Kovic, then, was the second bolt of lightning. Grievously wounded physically (he is paralyzed from the chest down), he said that Webb's speech had wounded him again. In addition to reopening some barely healed spiritual sores, Webb "represented the darkness and the evil that is growing in this country." Although he believed that James Webb was a compassionate man, to Ron Kovic he was also a horseman of the holocaust signaling the coming of "Amerika."

Although the balance of the remarks that afternoon weighed heavily against Webb, and the administration for which he was deemed to be a spokesman, there were many who were silent. It was not a silence, I think, that could be presumed to mean assent. Rather, it was a silence of pain, both for Kovic himself and for what he said. Frederick Downs served as a spokesman for this group when he rose to say, "I feel out of place here."

After the opening of such a cleavage, no one was in a place to speak for everyone. Few, however, could quarrel with David Winn's profoundly obvious observation, "America's soul is still split over Vietnam."

Following a public session that night at Cooper Union Great Hall, consisting of some very moving readings from their works by John Clark Pratt, Tim O'Brien, Ron Kovic, Wallace Terry, William Ehrhart, Robert Butler, and Bruce Weigl, the conference met again on Thursday morning (9 May) for the two final panels, one on the "Images of Asia and Asians in the Literature" and the other on "The Role of Literature in Understanding the War." The remarks of Al Santoli during the first panel produced the third lightning bolt. In contrast to Bill Ehrhart, for example, who had earlier said that America's intervention in Vietnam was an "unspeakable evil," Santoli fervently asserted that in attempting to preserve for the Vietnamese the option of an open society against the imposition of a brutal police state that characterizes Marxist-Leninist regimes of all stripes "my involvement in Vietnam was the proper thing to do." The subsequent history of Indochina, he felt, has clearly borne out the correctness of our intervention and of our current foreign policy toward the region. Through some very sharp interchanges, Santoli stuck to his insistence that the Vietnamese communists have imposed on their people a regime that conducts a Stalinist police state at home and a butchery of its neighboring Cambodians. This outcome was predictable during the Vietnam War, Santoli said, and it was not wrong to intervene to try to stop this from happening. During this third replay of the war debate, Arthur Egendorf was moved to remark, "I am surprised that in a conference on literature, talk of Asia is so concrete."

In the last panel the conference returned to a concluding discussion of the literature. It was here that the conference rose to the high level that made it such a success. This level of discussion could not have been achieved without the three lightning bolts. Each one risked wrecking the conference, but instead they each opened up, quite painfully, the avenues to building a new degree of understanding. The last session produced a real soul-searching, in part brought on by these exchanges. There was no catharsis, fortunately. After a catharsis, everyone comes together and all is forgotten. With the facts and the literature on Vietnam in such contention, any catharsis would have been a gloss, making the lessons as superficial as those bandied about now in national politics. This was not a superficial conference.

Instead the conference closed with some trenchant comments on the state of the Vietnam War literature and challenges for its future direction. Bill Broyles, the moderator, said he had been "exploring the geography of my heart a lot" and found in himself, and in the conference, "a confusion between the personal and the political." For Phil Beidler this confusion made it difficult to answer Thoreau's question, "How do you make a fact flower into a truth?" It is particularly difficult because to Myra MacPherson "the facts of the policymakers were some of the greatest fictions." The trouble is, though, for John Clark Pratt, "One man's fact is another man's fiction." Thus, to him, "there is no whole to the Vietnam experience."

Reflecting this, Pratt somberly acknowledged that he is made up of at least nine persons, all of whom were displayed at the conference. Like the literature, they do not add up to a totality, but consist of "fragments." These fragments cannot perceive the totality of the war, only its multiplicity. Such a literature cannot divine the truth, but it can present fragments of it and get the reader involved in the quest. The art form of this literature, in presenting a broken mosaic of fragments, is the collage. Arthur Egendorf was quick to observe that the conference itself was the embodiment of such a collage. Because the Vietnam War literature is illuminating these fragments, revealing the moral ambiguity that comes with them, James Chace concluded that it is "the most important literature being written right now."

From a literary perspective, one question that was addressed repeatedly throughout the conference was whether anyone was ready to, or capable of, writing the definitive work on Vietnam. Everyone who spoke on this question said they weren't, nor did they expect anyone else to try for some time. In the words of Jack Fuller, "I console myself with the fact that that's one question we can't answer now, and is not up to us to answer." What this conference revealed in the nearly universal rejection of any grand or transcendent vision above the fragmentary is that, even if such a definitive work has been written or is being written, America is not ready to read it.

In light of these stated affections for fragments and ambiguity, the value of these three lightning bolts in prodding the conference participants, I think, becomes clearer. James Webb, Ron Kovic, and Al Santoli tried to assert truths that most of their fellow participants weren't ready for: either to hear or to accept. The participants preferred, often quite vehemently, to hold on to the war as an ambiguity. In ambiguity, truth is provisional. In such a state, all egos can be intact, and in provisional harmony, because everyone might still be right even though they presently are in complete contradiction. The three lightning bolts forced the participants to define their ambiguities more clearly (and thereby start to peel them away) and confront some of their deepest aversions: for some, of the perhaps unexpected and terrible aftermaths of the war, and for others, whatever the conduct of the communists, of the undeniably duplicitous aspects of the American government's conduct of the war.

What also made this conference such a success was the mature way in which most of the participants responded to the three lightning bolts. The Asia Society is to be commended for bringing together a very sophisticated group of people. A large number of the participants had themselves written major works on the Vietnam War. This made the tenor of the discussion sober, thoughtful, and quite often humorous. The group itself was very diverse. There were novelists, poets, journalists, publishers, historians, and social scientists. This ensured that, while central direction was not lost, a range of issues arose that deflected participants from building up white heats of rage along a single line of argument. Also, ten years had passed since the end of the war. During the discussion in the last panel Al Santoli said that "Every person today has spoken from a sincere place." I'm not sure he would have said that five years ago, or even a year earlier. Both during and after the end of the war, enough people in the room had been through the futility of previous confrontations and shouting matches to see the wisdom of stepping back from further replays.

In addition to these more general factors, it would be remiss for me to fail to acknowledge the role of some key individuals who acted as healers with mollifying interventions at critical moments. The ones I specifically remember are Arthur Egendorf, Asa Baber, Tim O'Brien, and John Balaban. In this connection, one person for whom I cannot help but express my personal admiration is Colonel John W. Ripley, of the U.S.

Marines, the only person present at the conference in a military uniform. As a captain, John was awarded a Navy Cross for blowing up the bridge at Dong Ha in April 1972, seriously slowing the North Vietnamese advance into South Vietnam during the Easter Invasion. For his patient forbearance at the conference and for his restrained but fervent defense of the military profession as an honorable vocation, I think he earned the respect of everyone and deserves at least a second Navy Cross.

In my task of "writing this conference up," I have been charged with avoiding the Scylla of a lengthy string of transcribed excerpts without commentary and the Charybdis of a rambling essay of no discernible relation to the conference itself. Since the story of Scylla and Charybdis, taken from the perils of Ulysses' travels in the *Odyssey*, conveys such a tempestuous image, I would like to hope that what follows will convey more of the smooth harmony contained in the Oriental concepts of yin and yang.

My approach in this Mandate of The Asia Society (as distinct, I fear to point out, from Heaven) is to let the lightning bolts have their head, that is, to quote them fairly completely so that the shoals that the conference navigated between are well charted. For the bulk of the conference I will weave quotes and summaries around a description of the themes that dominated the conference: an examination of the Vietnam War literature, the tension between fact and fiction in this literature and in the authors, the images of Asians, and the literature's future direction and responsibility. Finally, I also will launch off on five essays that have grown out of my reflections on this conference in particular and on the literature on the war more generally: "The Crybaby Veterans," "What Are Facts?," "Reading the Asian Wind," "The *Iliad* and the *Kieu*: Building Understanding," and a concluding essay on "America's Future in Asia (and at Home)." Where a quoted excerpt is a full paragraph or longer, the speaker's name will be put at the start of the quote, and the quote itself will be indented slightly at the left margin. Otherwise, other people's remarks will be enclosed by quotation marks in the text. The text itself, then, can be taken as my summaries and commentaries. My longer essays will be marked by subtitles.

In his opening remarks to the conference Bob Oxnam said that he wanted "an open and candid expression" with a "purpose to yield light whether we achieve it by heat or other ways." There should be no doubt in Mr. Oxnam's mind that he got what he wanted. As to his purpose, I shall try to demonstrate this more slowly by organizing this "Mandate" in a progression from heat to light. Thus I start with the heat generated by James Webb's keynote speech, move on to the heat continued in Wednesday afternoon's two panels merged into the second chapter, "The Impact of the Literature: The High Tide of Passion," return to Wednesday morning's more dispassionate panels in a third chapter, "Down the Slippery Slope: Tensions Between Fiction and Fact." The fourth chapter raises the temperature again but in doing so reveals something of "The Great Lost Fact: The Asians." The fifth chapter, "Truth—Whither Goest Thou? The Role of the Literature in Understanding the War," assesses the amount of light the conference and the literature have shed on the Vietnam War thus far. The conclusion, "America's Future in Asia (and at Home)," goes beyond the bounds of the conference itself to discuss a larger context for an understanding of the Vietnam War, to wit, an assessment of the foreign policy of containment as part of the broader pattern of U.S.-Asian relations and an evaluation of existentialism in terms of its role in providing an intellectual framework for the existing literature on the Vietnam War.

1 The Keynote

"Artistic Resolution, Societal Resolution"

An issue that quickly came to the forefront at the conference was the separability of art and politics. During the war itself—in America and in Asia—nothing seemed separable from Vietnam. The war penetrated all. One man caught up in this "preoccupation" was the keynote speaker, James Webb. Like some others at the conference, Mr. Webb experienced heavy combat, in his case as a Marine captain in "I Corps," for which he was awarded a Navy Cross, a Silver Star, two Bronze Stars, and two Purple Hearts. Since the war he has found himself gripped by the tensions of translating his wartime experiences into the two contradictory worlds he now inhabits: the academy of the artist who writes novels and the orbit of the government official who makes policy. As an artist, Mr. Webb wrote the widely acclaimed *Fields of Fire* (1978), as well as *A Sense of Honor* (1981), a novel about a West Point cheating scandal. As a bureaucrat, he has, in his own words, served "three tours in government," currently as President Reagan's Assistant Secretary of Defense, Reserve Affairs. In his speech, quoted here in its entirety, the secretary underscored the tensions involved in interpreting the war from the conflicting perspectives of art and politics.

James Webb: I am not sure The Asia Society really comprehends what it has in this room: the tremendous brainpower, the diversity in experience and of opinions. I expect this to be a very lively few days.

It is a testament to the sensitivity over the divisions we still have on Vietnam that I have been asked to give a nonpolitical speech. This is almost an impossibility when one considers Vietnam and the mandate of the conference itself, but I'm going to try. I can't help but recall a conversation I had with one Mr. Hoan who runs the Vietnamese Embassy in Bangkok. I was in Bangkok three years ago trying to get into Vietnam to do a magazine story. I told Mr. Hoan I wanted to do a nonpolitical piece on the area where I had served. His answer in denying me my visa was that, "All events in life are political." I am also mindful of Plato's observation that "Art is politics." Given such agreement among members of one of the first free societies and one of the most recent closed systems, I can only demur, and promise you, in any event, I will try not to refight the Vietnam War.

The objective of this conference, according to the materials sent to me, is to explore some of the ways that literature has impacted on American perceptions of the Vietnam War, and to assess the longer-term impact on American perceptions of Asia as a whole, as well as the implication, and I think this is most important, for our country's future relations with Asia. The overriding desire of the conference, according to The Asia Society, is to sponsor a creative, forward-looking assessment of the long-term impact of this literature on our Asian relations. I congratulate The Asia Society for this creative approach to the pursuit of policy questions through the perspective of literature.

I've had an unusual career pattern for one whose principal occupation is that of a novelist in that I've spent three different tours in government. Government is, in many ways, directly opposed to art. In government it is necessary to boil down ambiguities, to make them "votable." It is essential that one make a concrete decision and take a tangible stand. If a government official believes that an issue is 51 percent correct, he must pull the lever or talk to the reporter, and justify his position. He is then on record. As the game is played, in many cases he must end up hardening his feelings about the other 49 percent that fell away when he made his decision.

This is a necessary way to run a government, but it is not the way to address problems rooted in the complexities of pain, lament, and tragedy. I learned quickly when I became the first Vietnam veteran to serve as counsel on the House Veterans Committee that we were not going to legislate away the problems of the veterans who served in the Vietnam War. The problems were too deep, too complex, and too filled with ambiguity—just as were the problems of our country as a whole when we were attempting to pick the scabs and examine the wounds from our decade of civil war known as the "Vietnam Era." It was for this reason that I wrote in the *Washington Post* in 1979, after covering the premiere of *Apocalypse Now*:

> Only the arts will provide resolution to our national angst over Vietnam. Only a good book or painting or play or movie can conjure the emotions and ambiguities of an experience, and through such exorcism affect attitudes that shape consciousness. We're seeing a good deal of art with respect to Vietnam, but very little of it has allowed us such emotional growth.
>
> Essence is a chemistry, a texture provided by sympathetically, or at least accurately, drawn characters in a state of mental conflict reaching for artistic resolution. If artistic resolution is reached, it can be allegorized into societal resolution. If it is false, the art form fails, along with the allegory.

So the good news is that through literature we can explore ambiguities and work toward synthesizing an enormously complex and painful experience. The bad news, at least from my perspective, is that our literature at this point gives us precious little grist for that particular mill. If anything, current American literature regarding the Vietnam era is too self-absorbed. It demonstrates how woefully little we understood the regional and global implications of our endeavor. American society is too often narcissistic and riddled with vicious domestic debate. At the same time, during the war it was romantic about the Vietnamese communists and completely ignorant, for the most part, about the implications of a North Vietnamese victory. In short, our writers, particularly those engaged in nonfiction, in many cases failed to prepare our society for the horrible results that followed the fall of Saigon. Nor have they yet given context for the changes in the region that followed the North Vietnamese victory.

I do not say this with malice, but rather to state my reservations at the outset of this conference regarding the effectiveness of our literature to date in meeting the mandate of this conference. We have a number of very good combat narratives which testify in many cases to a policy gone awry, to the difficulty of fighting an enemy in populated areas, and to the lack of understanding generated by our nineteen-year-old warriors toward an Asian culture. A discussion of these narratives and of their themes will be helpful, and I expect may even mitigate many of the negative perceptions that still exist.

In a conference dedicated to the future in Asia—and I must say that the future of America is very much in Asia: our balance of trade shows this as does the productivity in those countries that have been able to remain free—I would ask participants to consider the situation in Southeast Asia today, and compare it against the contents of the many major award-winning works published during and immediately after the war.

First, as we all know, the pure flame of the revolution did not burn after 1975 in Vietnam. South Vietnam, Cambodia, and Laos were conquered. Two million Cambodians are dead. No South Vietnamese were brought into high positions in the new government. At least one million Vietnamese have fled. Sixty-five thousand South Vietnamese soldiers, mostly officers, the leadership of the South Vietnamese army, are estimated to have died in reeducation camps. Vietnam now has the fourth largest army in the world with one million men under arms. Fifty thousand Vietnamese soldiers occupy Laos. One hundred sixty thousand occupy Cambodia.

Just as importantly, the Russians for the first time in their history have warm water ports in the Pacific. The Soviet Pacific fleet is twice as large as our own Pacific fleet, numbering more than 450 vessels. These vessels are new and very capable ships, many geared for offensive operations, including helicopter carriers and amphibious landing craft. On any given day, twenty-two Soviet ships operate out of Cam Ranh Bay, as do Badger and Backfire bombers, Bear reconnaissance aircraft, and MIG-23 fighters. This is not a political observation; it is a factual one.

Additionally, we have seen our war veterans depicted repeatedly as aberrants—as men without values dragged into the war zone against their will, later as losers, finally as victims—while the facts have too often demonstrated otherwise. Every unit had its problem children, its "Phonies" if I may extract from *Fields of Fire*. But too often our literature has made them the norm. Statistics show that:

- two-thirds of our Vietnam era veterans were volunteers,
- three-fourths of the combat dead were, in fact, volunteers,
- 91 percent were glad they served their country,
- and 74 percent enjoyed their time in the military.

They also indicate that a Vietnam veteran is:

-less likely to be in jail than his nonveteran counterpart,
-no more likely to use drugs,
-more likely to have gone to college,
-more likely to be married, and
-more likely to own a home.

Furthermore, according to a recent *Washington Post*–ABC News survey, Vietnam veterans felt they benefited from their service in Vietnam by a margin of two-to-one, 88 percent supported the bombing of North Vietnam, two-thirds support the use of napalm, and a two-to-one plurality agreed with Westmoreland's handling of the war.

Too often a character embodying these qualities in our literature —volunteer, the usual aspirations, supportive of the basic policy if not of the craziness that is apparent in all wars—is the foil, the fall guy, the one who "does not understand."

I do not wish to criticize any work merely because it disagreed with government policy. Nor do I wish to imply that our writers should have been prophets as well as commentators. Although I personally agree with the validity of our effort in Vietnam, I also believe it was our flawed government policy that made the war unwinnable, and therein pierced us through our national soul. Moreover, we are the most self-critical society on earth, and this is our greatest strength. We are multicultural; we have varying moral references on any important issue; we are incurably idealistic; and most importantly, we have the luxury, through our system of government, to engage in what Justice Oliver Wendell Holmes once termed, "the open air of free debate."

But the sad reality is that the debate, even given the improvement in publishing over the past two years or so, has neither been full, nor, to be honest, completely fair about what we were attempting to do in Vietnam. There are a number of reasons for this. One is the overall volatility of the Vietnam era in areas larger than the war. Another is the nature of what we might call the artistic soul. A third is the chemistry of the arts and journalistic community as it relates to our government.

With respect to the first, if we are to draw conclusions about the impact of the war on Asia and on its future, our friends in Asia deserve an effort on our part to separate out the dynamics of the many domestic issues that dovetailed into the Vietnam protest years. As we all well remember, the '60s and the '70s in this country were volatile in more areas than merely Vietnam, and a good deal of the turmoil attributed to the war actually carried spillover from these other areas. We should not forget, for instance, that the Civil Rights Act and the Gulf of Tonkin Resolution were both signed in the summer of 1964, and that the war's peak during Tet '68 and the bitter rioting following Martin Luther King's assassination were only about two months apart. In fact, the Students for a Democratic Society was formed before there even was a Vietnam War, with the notion that race, not war, would provide the basis for revolution in this country. The implications of this thinking were clear in many leaders of the antiwar movement. Jerry Rubin did not say he was going to end the war when he led the march on the Pentagon in October 1967. He said, "We are now in the business of wholesale and widespread resistance, and the dislocation of American society." As another example, there was a direct nexus between the collapse of the Nixon administration from Watergate and the sudden collapse of the South Vietnamese nation. Where appropriate, such issues need to be removed from our analysis. Where relevant, and when they indicate a sea change in American political views, they should be included.

Second, consider the artist himself. He or she is dedicated to analyzing the human condition. He reacts to pain and tragedy. He seeks what we call the truth, which normally transcends politics and yet is riddled with ambiguities. It is the glory of art that it does not have to boil down these ambiguities, that it can leave the 51 percent as it stands, and not be required to justify the lack of consensus. On occasion, art has profound political impact as, for instance, Arthur Koestler's masterpiece, *Darkness at Noon*. But more often than not, the artist sets himself against the agents of suffering and on the side of those who are now its victims. This sometimes takes on a romantic view that does not consider long-term impacts, and even greater potential suffering.

Finally, take into account the writer's community. Perhaps the most precious freedom in our society is the right to question government authority. Our intellectual community is by its very nature the adversary of government. Eisenhower warned of the "Military-Industrial Complex," but did not consider that its counter was, for lack of a better term, the "Academic-Intellectual Complex."

In media and publishing circles, supporting government policy of almost any sort in this country becomes akin to selling out. Such a writer is quite often viewed by his peers and by critics to be either stupid or a pawn. Awards are lavished on those who discover new ways to question or attack government policy, to tell us where our government is failing us. In many cases, this is why we are so politically dynamic. This is good. In others, however, it amounts to false bravado, and a wrongheaded intimidation of those who believe government policy has been misunderstood. The end result is that we need more openness, and a more varied literature. Sometimes it takes more courage to confront the hostility of one's peers than it does to attack that amorphous dragon called government policy. The arts will provide us our much needed societal resolution only if the forum is open so that the debate is real.

Vietnam was many things. It varied year by year, place by place, unit by unit. No one reporting it or remembering it is without predisposition. We as artists are like blind men stroking the elephant, calling out our impressions to our readers so that they can compile them and come up with a larger picture. But it would do no good to deny one man the right, for instance, to report that the elephant had tusks. If one position is filtered, or diluted, or denied legitimacy before it reaches the public, then not only is the debate false but the damage is greater than if the debate had not occurred at all, since we will have provided a false illusion that the debate did take place.

As you discuss the body of works that are available for analysis, compare it against the facts that have been slowly emerging over the last decade. And ask yourselves about the literature that is still waiting in the wings for its proper recognition. The present literature is in many cases memorable. But consider whether it fully represents the dynamics of this complex and painful experience.

Our future is indeed in Asia. It does us no good to distort the past, or to block the realities of the present, as we reach for greater harmony in that vital region.

Discussion

It can be safely said that following Mr. Webb's address people did not simply push back their chairs, chew betel nut, and languidly prepare their stomachs for rest. Mr. Webb, instead, was quickly beset by "fields of fire" that triggered an energetic discussion encapsulating and setting the stage for all the themes that were pursued subsequently in the conference: politics, facts and statistics, who was hurt more by the vagaries of publishing, the forgotten Asians, and the role of the literature.

It was Jim Webb's politics that drew first fire. Accompanied by applause, Bill Ehrhart opened up with, "I am sorry your speech was so political. What I saw and did in Asia in thirteen months was unspeakably evil and immoral. What is happening there now does not change that. And what the Vietnamese are doing now; well, they are not doing it in my name or with my tax dollar. They are not asking me to pull the trigger."

Pursuing this theme of the war as evil, Bob Butler contended, "The writers in this room are prophets in that they see things that the majority of the people do not. What these writers have seen [in Vietnam] is the true evil." The evil, however, may spread beyond the United States. Bill Broyles, a moderator for one of the panels, made a recent return journey to Vietnam. Writing in the April 1985 issue of the *Atlantic Monthly*, he related a discussion with a group of European diplomats in Hanoi quibbling over the foibles of the new socialist regime. One of them suddenly turned to Broyles, "All this is just bureaucracy. What matters is that they are evil, truly evil."

During this discussion on Webb's speech, though, most who spoke preferred to criticize American foreign policy. Joe Klein, in harkening back to Webb's remark that the literature on the war is narcissistic, thought that it was "the ultimate in narcissism to, ten years later, try to justify a policy that was essentially misguided." Lady Borton suggested that the real reason for the flow of one million refugees from Indochina was not the establishment of communist regimes but the "very astringent American foreign policy" that followed their establishment. In cutting off all aid to Vietnam on April 30, 1975, the United States, "cut off their Hondas and put the Saigonnese back to the age of the bicycle." So they fled. James Harrison, in taking Webb to task for exaggerating the extent of Hanoi's threat to Southeast Asia, asked him, in any case, "Does anything surprise you about what is happening now in Vietnam? Why can't the U.S. government talk to them and open up relations?" Mr. Webb responded by saying he did not want to engage Harrison in a big debate, but what he had said about the postwar realities were simple facts.

But James Webb's simple facts and statistics were even more contentious to many in the group than the foreign policy based upon them. The most offensive statistic, and one that came up again and again in the conference, was the 91 percent: the 91 percent of the Vietnam veterans who were glad they served their country. Myra MacPherson, who has just completed a major study of Vietnam veterans, was particularly concerned about this figure. "I'm worried about the 91 percent," she said. She had read the same study and found, for example, that 33 percent of these same veterans expressed qualms about their military service. "It is wrong," then, "to keep using this 91 percent statistic." Webb defended his statistics by saying they came from a $6 million Harris Poll commissioned by the Veterans Administration, which was the most comprehensive survey ever done of Vietnam veterans. MacPherson persisted, though, by insisting that you have to differentiate between pride in service and the very ambiguous feelings many veterans had as to why they were there. She, in turn, cited the *Washington Post*'s "Vietnam Legacy" study that revealed enormous ambiguities among veterans across a wide spectrum of issues. There then followed this exchange:

Webb: Are you going to give validity to a statistical sampling, or not?
MacPherson: I have great doubts . . .
Someone (in the back, interrupting and shouting): No.
Webb: No . . . . Then no poll means anything.

Joe Klein offered the results of his own small survey of twenty veterans instead. Of the twenty, 100 percent were proud they had served in the military, but zero percent could answer any of his questions with a straight "yes" or "no" answer. To this, James Webb the novelist admitted, "Well, truth is ambiguous." In fact, his own 91 percent statistic is tinged with some. A look at his survey itself shows that in response to the statement: "Looking back, I am glad I served my country," 73 percent said it matched their feelings "very closely" and 18 percent said it matched their feelings "somewhat closely." Combined, this makes 91 percent, but one can imagine a rainbow of opinions streaming into the bucket of "somewhat closely" and even some range into "very closely."

Following the Webb-MacPherson exchange, Bill Broyles rose and, to great applause, observed, "This seems to me to be a silly debate." He then cited a survey of veterans of World War II, the good war without ambiguities, in which 48 percent found their military experience to be negative. "People who really like their war experiences—good war or bad war—have serious problems," he concluded amid much laughter and applause. In bringing up the World War II comparison, to Webb this only underscored the fact that combat itself is an intensely apolitical environment. In a controversial war like Vietnam the unique burden on the Vietnam veteran is that he is asked to justify his combat experience, and he is not prepared or equipped to do so. It is, concluded Webb, an unfair burden. After this, the debate on this issue subsided.

The next issue that arose provoked a confusing cross fire over which ideological perspective on the war was more discriminated against by the publishing industry. In response to Bob Butler's assertion that no true prophet could write anything about Vietnam reflecting Webb's 91 percent statistic, Webb replied that he thought there were people writing books more representative of the Veterans Administration's survey, but that their books weren't being published. For his own *Fields of Fire* he encountered problems over his views with the editors of nine publishers. Until two years ago, Webb contended, it was very difficult to get anything published "that did not genuflect before the negation of the war."

Looking at the publishing industry more generally, Bill Broyles reflected, "I am not sure that's true."

Fred Downs, in his words, "speaking for a Midwestern point of view," insisted that what Webb said about publishing *was* true. In the case of Downs's book anyway, his agent told him, "my book wasn't antiwar enough." *Playboy* magazine said, "I didn't apologize enough." Another publisher wrote, "I did not exhibit enough guilt." Arthur Egendorf seconded Downs. He related his experience in getting a book published as mirroring what both Webb and Downs had said. People in the publishing industry have very hardened opinions against the war, he contended. "Well," demanded Abe Peck, "Where was this liberal antiwar publishing establishment when I needed them?" Although hardly a central flash point, this cross fire over publishing discrimination sputtered on for the duration of the conference.

There was one salvo of Jim Webb's that went largely unanswered. Regardless of perspective, he reminded the group that the literature of the Vietnam War still does not represent the full parameters of the conflict, particularly the Asian dimensions. He asked the question, "What can we contribute to our Asian friends?" and answered, "Very little right now." Lady Borton put her finger on part of it: "One main problem is that we are talking about a place and we are not talking about people. Our future is with Asians and that includes both the fleeing boat people and the Vietnamese still in Vietnam." Bill Broyles touched on another. In response to Webb's criticism of the literature's failure to confront what is going on in Vietnam, he explained that this is "very difficult because the experience of the Vietnamese is closed to us . . . . You are asking people to evoke, in art, experiences which were in reality very distant."

The only demurrer to Webb's criticism came from Joe Klein: "I hear statements like our future is in Asia. I think our future is in America, and statements like this get us into trouble." Clearly Joe Klein is not the only American who finds an examination of post-1975 Indochina to be uncomfortable, and an "experience," therefore, that has been largely avoided. This reluctance did cause trouble later on in the conference—in the person of Al Santoli and his verbal bludgeoning of the conference with these postwar realities.

Interspersed throughout this skirmishing *were* some moments of sober reflection on the literature itself that prefigured some of the fine discussion in the conference's final session. Bill Broyles led off by saying, "We are at the stage in the Vietnam literature where personal experience is still the real root of what most people have been writing about." Though this may be true, Fred Downs pointed out that the literature is now getting on to the next stage. "What Jim said about the facts and figures is real," he said. "As writers, we're directing people's thoughts into channels. Unless we look at the consequences of the things Jim talked about, we're not communicating."

Phil Beidler hoped that, with the politicization of the Vietnam War and all the scrutiny it was coming under as a result, we might be the first nation to learn something from history, and that this literature might be able to help. In this regard, Joseph Ferrandino pressed Jim Webb on whether he felt the Vietnam literature "has contributed to the reluctance of the administration to commit troops to other areas of the globe?" Jim was reluctant to agree. "I'm not sure the literature itself has." Rather, it's more the societal experience of the war that might have contributed to this. As he said, "We've all grown up in the war. There is no one who has been involved in Vietnam whether to fight in it, or to fight the war, who doesn't have something to feel bad about, or to feel beat up about." The most beat-up element is the U.S. military. "It is a very badly wounded establishment," he contended. As for lessons, though, the literature, Webb said, has not yet provided the larger context necessary for drawing lessons.

If the literature cannot yet draw lessons, it may, as Bob Butler affirmed, aspire to prophecy. With some violation to the evening's actual chronology, I will close this discussion with Arthur Egendorf's short treatise on prophecy. It drew by far the most applause of the evening.

Egendorf: With respect to prophecy, I don't see how one understands the past more fully without implying a view toward the future. The two are inseparable. Every interpretation of the past is an implicit prophecy. The question for us at this conference is: what are we prophesying? We should be prophesying about America's vocation. What is our new vocation in the globe? In the new millennium, is our vocation to contain Soviet power? Is this the calling to the American spirit?

I don't think so. Our future is in Asia. Walt Whitman, a long time ago, said our future is in Asia. So what is the East for us, and what did die in Vietnam? Was it a bad policy, or notions of America's vocation?

Webb: Thank you. Well said.

No "artistic resolution" or "societal resolution" occurred in this evening's discussion or in the conference generally, but James Webb, as the keynote speaker, did provide the spark for a very lively few days.

2 The High Tide of Passion

The Impact of the Literature

I feel out of place here. —*Fred Downs, conference participant*

If every point has a counterpoint and every action an opposite reaction, the opposite reaction to James Webb's keynote address came on the afternoon of the conference's second day. The shocks or the lightning bolts came in three pulses. Each pulse rose to a brink from the surges of Ron Kovic's impassioned speeches. The first, on "Wounds," touched off a discussion on the plight of the veteran in American society. The second, in response to a question about the Vietnam Memorial, sparked a denunciation by Kovic of the government and a warning that a Nazi America may be upon us. Although something like 91 percent of the participants seemed to be swept along in these tides, most did step back from this prognosis of fascism. Nevertheless, his incendiary words kindled a brushfire of political outbursts. Kovic's final speech contained something of a plea for national and personal reconciliation. With this, the flood of passion ebbed, and the afternoon's deliberations returned to the anguish of the veterans and the divisive impact of the war on American society.

In portraying the controversies of the afternoon, I have built my story around Ron Kovic's three outbursts. In so doing I have done considerable violence to the chronology of the discussion and even rearranged the ordering of Kovic's speeches to separate out the three themes. If literal accuracy is the victim of this process, I hope the essential spirit of the afternoon in clearer terms is the beneficiary.

For the record, though, the structure of the afternoon's session on the "Literature on the War's Impact on a Generation of Americans" was built on two panels. The first, on the "Literature on the Vietnam Experience," was moderated by Joseph Farrandino of Columbia University. His panelists were William Ehrhart (*Vietnam—Perkasie*, 1983), Joe Klein (*Payback*, 1984), and Ron Kovic (*Born on the Fourth of July*, 1976). The panelists for the second, on "The Impact of Those at Home," were C. D. B. Bryan (*Friendly Fire*, 1976), Myra MacPherson (*Long Time Passing: Vietnam and the Haunted Generation*, 1985), and David Winn (*Gangland*, 1982). Its moderator was Abe Peck of Northwestern University.

To begin, the sense of Joe Farrandino's agenda paper and opening remarks as a panel moderator were that for most veterans the Vietnam War still rages on "over here" as they struggle to adjust to "the world" and to control and to understand their own feelings about the war and their participation in it. If Ron Kovic represents nothing else, he is a living embodiment of this struggle.

Lightning Bolt II   The Wound

Ron Kovic: I'd like to first respond to something that wounded me very deeply last night. I patiently sat in the back of the room as James Webb began his keynote address. I began to realize that something very dangerous was happening . . . there was an attempt to undo everything that I and others had done. This man, in a very insensitive and callous fashion, was trying to negate my suffering, and the suffering of thousands and thousands of Americans and Vietnamese.

I was very upset. I felt physically wounded. I felt my wound come back to me. I was shot on January 20, 1968, through the right foot and the right shoulder. The bullet that hit my shoulder went through my lung and it severed my spinal cord, paralyzing me for life. It's taken me almost eighteen years to come to terms with my paralysis. I'm paralyzed from my mid-chest down—I can't feel or move anything from my chest down. I will never be able to walk again, or to make love. But I'm not complaining to you. I'm telling you that I'm strong and that I have my life together now. I feel a wholeness that I never believed in 1968 I would ever be able to feel.

That one speech last night drove deep into that wholeness, wounded me again, and allowed me to feel the weight of my injuries. I'm very proud of everybody here in the room—I'm very proud of all of you —and this talk last night: it tried to demean the precious and courageous and beautiful and sensitive and compassionate and compelling work that has been achieved by the authors in this room. I was very saddened and wounded. I looked to the person next to me and I said, "I'm feeling hurt again. I'm feeling wounded again." Then I turned to the person once more and I said, "No. You know what? I'm feeling America's wound. And I'm feeling how deep and grievous it is."

I wasn't angry at Jim. I was sad because this wound has not healed. It may never heal.

So the veterans suffer, and America—sometimes—suffers with them. It started, really, when they first came home in unnoticeable driblets while the war still went on. Bill Ehrhart's poem "Coming Home" captures this "first" suffering admirably:

San Francisco airport—
no more corpsmen stuffing ruptured chests
with cotton balls and not enough heat tabs
to eat a decent meal.
I asked some girl to sit
and have a Coke with me.
She thought I was crazy.
I thought she was going to call a cop.
I bought a ticket for Philadelphia.
At the loading gate, they told me:
"Thank you for flying TWA;
we hope you will enjoy your flight."
No brass bands;
no flags,
no girls,
no cameramen.
Only a small boy who asked me
what the ribbons on my jacket meant.

What was so cruelly disillusioning about this almost nonevent of coming home is that for many GI's, while they were in Vietnam, this promised moment of coming home was their grip on sanity. As one writer put it, "they counted their days to DEROS [Date of Estimated Return from Overseas] like a metronome." That the craziness of the war might continue in some other form at home was unthinkable. For Arthur Egendorf, whose educational level was certainly a cut above that of the average G.I. in Vietnam, his return to the United States was like the end of Ulysses' wanderings in the *Odyssey:* to the bliss of Penelope's waiting arms or, in Arthur's case, to the certitude of his antiwar views. But in his graduate studies he came upon a sequel to the *Odyssey* by Nikos Kazantzakis in which Ulysses finds he cannot stay at home, that his quest must continue: that for Ulysses, gone for so long, there was no home anymore. This forced Arthur into a turbulent reexamination of the "home" of his antiwar position, a turbulence that continues.

In his book, *Payback* (1984), Joe Klein traced the lives of five marines for fifteen years from the battles they shared in "Operation Cochise" in 1967 through *their* turbulent reentry into American society. Their problems were twofold: Home—"the world"—had changed, but so had they. Individually, this awkward interaction described what psychiatrists came to call Post-traumatic Stress Disorder. Nationally, this incapacitation became, more simply, the Vietnam Syndrome. For the generation of the 1960s, institutions were breaking apart, belief systems were being searchingly reexamined, life-styles were changing, and with them values were being set adrift. No one was putting down any anchors. For Joe Stein, one of Klein's veterans, the language had even lost its meaning. The beauty queen being interviewed on TV said Vietnam was a "downer" and that "the guys who went to Canada are the real heroes. The guys who went to Vietnam are just a bunch of baby-killers and murderers." "The world" had turned topsy-turvy.

But the veterans weren't the same either. They waded ashore onto the beaches of Danang bolstered by the bravado and moral certainty of John Wayne. But John Wayne never played too well in Vietnam. Being the good guy, a seemingly prerequisite antecedent for outbursts of American ferocity, was an image that always had problems coming into focus in Vietnam. As Fred Downs put it: "One of the problems was the moral code with which we were brought up. We needed justification for what we were doing. We never got the reassurance." As Joe Klein related, it was a real release for many veterans to say many years later, "Screw John Wayne!" But the passion of these outbursts, if they ever came, were puzzling to the stay-at-home civilians. To the wizened child of the '60s, John Wayne may have been irrelevant, and even slightly ridiculous, but worthy of a derisive curse!? There was a gap.

The pain of this gap upon coming home, I am sure, can be felt by every veteran who reads Bill Ehrhart's poem, "Imagine":

> The conversation turned to Vietnam.
> He'd been there, and they asked him
> what it had been like:
> had he been in battle?
> Had he ever been afraid?
> Patiently, he tried to answer
> questions he had tried to answer
> many times before.
> They listened, and they strained
> to visualize the words:
> newsreels and photographs, books
> and Wilfred Owen tumbled
> through their minds.
> Pulses quickened.
> They didn't notice, as he talked,
> his eyes, as he talked,
> his eyes begin to focus
> through the wall, at nothing,
> or at something inside.
> When he finished speaking,
> someone asked him:
> had he ever killed?

To avoid the social hell of such a question, many Vietnam veterans turned deeply inward, keeping their anguish bottled up, and hid themselves from a society that was ignoring them anyway. Myra MacPherson, in her study of Vietnam veterans, was able to prize open the lids holding down these deeply held feelings. The differences, both among veterans themselves and between some of her interviewees' public selves and privately held feelings, startled her. One of her most poignant examples was Gerry. Publicly, Gerry was a fireman in a small town in Alabama where he recalled Vietnam as a noble cause and espoused fervently anticommunist views. Privately, his feelings of alienation and betrayal had been so intense that he suffered a nervous breakdown before joining the fire department. The end of her long study of this "haunted Vietnam generation" is that there will be no healing until there is first an airing and then a reconciling of these often deeply buried feelings.

In the last few years America has begun to gingerly peek at its Vietnam veterans, and at "their" war. The Vietnam Memorial unveiled in Washington, D.C., has served as a symbol of this belated recognition. For some, the Memorial (as well as more recent ones in cities like New Orleans, New York, and Boston) has provided the opportunity for catharsis and a letting go of pent-up emotions and nightmarish memories. But it is the doom of everything connected with Vietnam to be controversial. So it has been with the Memorial itself. Some don't like the design. Some didn't like it that there were no figures or flags, and some are upset that none of the figures is female. Now that there are figures and flags, some don't like the flags. Some objections are brief. Bill Ehrhart said, "What does it reveal in terms of the Veterans' experience? In my opinion, I would have to honestly answer, nothing." Others have a longer list of objections. Ron Kovic's was biting, bitter, and full of rage.

Lightning Bolt II   The Rage

Ron Kovic: When I saw the wall for the first time, I said, "My God, 58 thousand American boys killed because of the United States Government's foreign policy." Fifty-eight thousand killed because they lied to us, because they used us, because they fed us with all this crap about John Wayne and being a hero and the romance of war and everything we watched on television. They set up my generation, they set us up for that war. They made us believe that war was going to be something glorious and something beautiful, just like they set up the veterans of World War I. The bands were playing. Everybody told us to go.

We had been the children of the Second World War. The Children, and we had gone without question. Many of us believed, and I have in the beginning of my book John F. Kennedy's January 20th, 1961, inaugural address, "Ask not what your country can do for you, but what you can do for your country." Millions of us were deeply touched by what John F. Kennedy said on that January day in 1961. I sat in my living room at 227 Toronto Avenue in Massapequa and tears streamed down my face because I felt that I had a purpose in my life. I felt that I had an obligation to serve my country. And I was used, and that's one of the great torments of that war. All of this youth and beauty and life and all of this intelligence, and we were innocent. We really became intelligent when we realized that we had been used, and that our generation had been crushed by their madness and their lies and their ignorance.

When I see that wall, I see beautiful young men, I see sensitive men, I see high school graduates. I scc myself on that goddamn wall and my whole generation plastered up there. I think about the twelve friends I have on that wall and how they'll never be able to say the things that I am saying right now. Did you ever think for a moment, did you ever think for one moment in your life, what would they say? What would the dead on that wall say? If they could speak, what would they say? "Gee whiz, I really love it here. It's really great being dead. It's really great being in the ground at 21 and not being able to breathe or to make lôve or to have a life." What if the dead could speak, because who speaks for the dead in this country? The government speaks for the dead.

There is a part of me that wants to leave, that wants to get out of here, that wants to go to another country, that wants to become an expatriate, because it just becomes too painful sometimes to watch this Nazification of my country. It's 1938; it's not 1985. It's 1938 and somebody's burning books. They're burning *The Road Back* by Erich Remarque. They're burning *All Quiet on the Western Front*. Thcy're burning all the antiwar literature of World War I because Hitler wants to do it again. Maybe Hitler is in the White House right now. Maybe there are those of you who want to continue to live in Disneyland, to continue to feel that maybe it's all gonna work out o.k. in the end. Maybe it is gonna be a nice ending. I feel sometimes like I want to leave.

Let me lastly say that the wall stirs up deep emotions for all of us, and everyone will have their own interpretation of that wall. I was with Jan Scruggs [one of the directors of the Vietnam Memorial project] the other night. We did a television show together and I thanked him. I thanked him and I thank you [John Wheeler, the questioner of Kovic and another director of the project] for putting that wall up. I thank you for reminding all of us of our generation. I have only one criticism: that the words, "never again, never again," were not put above the names on that wall so that we do not kill another generation and we do not repeat the madness and insanity and the callous disregard for youth. Are we going to learn, are we going to grow, are we going to repeat it again? What kind of country is this, if we would ever let it happen again?

Following upon Kovic's second outburst, many other believers shed their artistic clothing and rebaptized themselves in the bile of the Vietnam War's politics. C. D. B. Bryan made his point by telling the story of a Memorial Day observance in Stoney Creek, Connecticut, in which the townspeople, for America's bicentennial, did not want their dead forgotten, but were not too keen on yielding up any more of their sons to war. There is a lesson in all this memorializing he felt.

> **Bryan:** It is our responsibility to make sure that those who lead us don't have the arrogance of those who led us through that [Vietnam] period. We must celebrate what is best about America, which is, us, the people, and not those men who led us and lied to us so badly —and not to let it happen again.

Unfortunately, as Myra MacPherson has acknowledged, the Vietnam era generation is a "mishmash." Some are like Ron Kovic, C. D. B. Bryan, and Bill Ehrhart, and never want "it" to happen again. But there are others who are *cheerily* urging "it" to happen again. Among those in the latter camp, the ones who are particularly galling to Myra MacPherson, are men who never served in Vietnam yesterday but are today embracing a course of bellicose intervention in Nicaragua. A sterling example, according to her, is Chris Buckley, son of the famous "superhawk" editor of *National Review,* who was "quietly for the war" during his years of military eligibility, and now that he is "over the hill" is publicly endorsing aid to the *contras.*

Artists, like everyone else, have their agendas, and the pull of using their art in the service of their message, in the case of Vietnam, comes almost as a moral imperative. With his characteristic and admirable honesty, Bill Ehrhart, the poet, ironically like James Webb before him, confessed to the politics of his art.

> **Ehrhart:** I find it extremely difficult to sit here and talk about the Vietnam War as art. I don't give a goddamn about art. I'm not an artist. I'm an educator, and my writing is a tool of education. I think I feel as strongly as Ron does that, if I cannot affect the course of my country as a result of my experiences, then whatever I do as a writer is an utter failure.

With most of the conference participants now bowing before Plato's ancient wisdom that "art is politics," there were those in the conference who still hung back from joining in the spirit of Kovic's denunciations. This hesitancy was not out of greater artistic purity but because of differences with his politics.

Joe Klein offered the hope that the stirrings of a national reconciliation were beginning. Despite his deep personal admiration for Ron Kovic, Joe recoiled from the Nazification of America part. "I think it really is reckless, Ron, to talk about Nazi Germany. I think that as writers we have to be a little more precise with our words. This isn't Nazi Germany. It isn't even close," he admonished. Joe also felt that perhaps the extent of the changes wrought by the 1960s has been exaggerated. For all the turbulence of the period, most of the veterans returned to settings similar to what they had known before, and most of the veterans themselves were pretty much "the same old clunks like everybody else, like all the generations that had come before." And now the kids are even coming up to them and asking them to tell war stories.

Also standing at the water's edge was Fred Downs. As a wounded veteran himself, but also as a personal friend of James Webb, the tenor of the afternoon's discussion moved him to say, "I feel out of place here. As a writer," he contended, "I whittle away at the truth through introspection. But this process requires a back and forth between two points of view." He didn't find more than one point of view being represented here, and he wondered how useful it was to hear yet another batch of antiwar tirades that have been going on for eighteen years like a tired liturgy. The quest for authors to pursue was not to mope around and lash themselves to death but to answer the question, "How are we going to recover?"

Another one standing to the side was Bill Broyles. He admitted to being powerfully affected by both James Webb and Ron Kovic—and very disturbed. What disturbed him was that both asserted such concrete and very certain political generalities about what we should do as a country in light of their experiences in a war that is still mired in ambiguity. That their prescriptions are so totally opposite is the best demonstration of this ambiguity. Despite the undeniable validity of Kovic's own suffering, Broyles said, it is dangerous to generalize from one's own sufferings. He pointed out that the British, for example, lost more men in the first month of the Battle of the Somme in World War I (including 20,000 killed on the first day) than we lost in the entire Vietnam War, and yet the British, despite this appalling suffering, went on to fight in World War II, and few would fault the British for doing so. Also, he observed that in C. D. B. Bryan's

Memorial story, despite the suffering inflicted on the British soldier Billy's family by the patriots of Stoney Creek, if Billy hadn't been killed, we still might be in the British Empire. Thus, to Broyles the ambiguity of this conflict between individual suffering and collective welfare is what literature should examine and illuminate.

Whatever his politics, what was genuine about Ron Kovic, and what spoke to all the conference participants, was his anguish—and plea for reconciliation.

Lightning Bolt II   The Reconciliation?

Ron Kovic: I wrote a poem once, "After the war there was no God, and for Him there was no country anymore." There was very little left of a country for me. There was very little left of a mother and a father and sisters and brothers, family; the war shattered all of that. There was just me, alive and breathing every single day, trying to make sense of this madness. What does it mean to really be dead, to lose everything, because I don't believe in God. There is no God for me after Vietnam.

Yeah, I feel very alone, very alienated from my country, from my mother, from my father, from my friends. I feel two things: I want people to feel what I'm feeling. I want people to act the way I want to act. I want people to feel the urgency that I feel. I want to feel a part of everyone else, even while sitting in a wheelchair. I'm convinced that I can feel a part of everyone else.

I marched with the veterans, thousands of veterans the other day. I was in Washington, D.C., speaking from the Capitol to 75,000 people who don't want another Vietnam. I was at Columbia University a week ago with young students who weren't even born when Vietnam happened. All of them want one thing. They want peace, they want decency, they want a sensitive country, they want a caring country, a compassionate country.

We all have different visions. But I'm telling you that part of me is hopeful, part of me believes, part of me is confident that this new nation, this new world, is going to come into being. And it's going to be a beautiful place. It's not a Utopian thought. It's a practical reality and we can do it. We can do it. We have it within ourselves to all come together.

I'm closer to loving James Webb than I am to hating him. I don't want to hate Jim, and I don't want to hate President Reagan. I want to believe, as Martin Luther King and as Gandhi would believe, that it is better to love than to hate. And the side of me that I think has sway right now is this hopeful side. Isn't that wonderful, that someone could be hit so hard, could have so much taken away, to be raped as Mr. Bryan said . . . and still tell you eighteen years later . . . that he is still hopeful, that he is still hopeful, that he still believes!

I love James Webb. I feel we are very close. I respect James Webb. I want to be able to hold him in my arms and embrace him as a comrade, as a friend, as a fellow American, a fellow human being. I have great hope for this country. I believe. But we have to risk, and we have to challenge, and we have to show . . . [that] to let this [Vietnam] happen again, for those young boys from Massapequa who I'm going to speak to at Massapequa High School next week, for them to have to be devastated and crushed the way my generation was crushed, would be an obscenity. . . .

We have to change as human beings. We have to put people first, human beings first. I think James Webb and myself would agree that people are important, and that life is precious, and that our literature should respect all of those things.

Can we learn to love each other so much, as Ron Kovic seems to suggest, that wars will cease? Colonel John Ripley, of the U.S. Marines, rose to the floor to say that we couldn't. He warned that we can't draw lessons from our personal experiences and our emotions. National policy can't be made from statements based only on individual experiences. They'll be too contradictory and clouded with emotion. To go a step further from these emotions, as some did, and make the statement, "Never again, never again," is absolute nonsense, the colonel insisted. "It's fruitless and hopeless to think that this country will never again be involved in some sort of conflict." The recognition of the inevitability of conflict goes back a long way. Colonel Ripley thought it was Plato who said, "Only the dead have seen the end to war."

As for the men who fought with Colonel Ripley in Vietnam, he said, "We didn't ask for the war. Nevertheless, we fought the war, and we saw honor and dignity in what we were doing." To those bereaved by America's dead, he felt that no words could offer better comfort than those of General Douglas MacArthur:

> For those men who were lost, I cannot tell you the humble origins of their birth, but I can tell you the tremendous honor and dignity of their deaths. We don't know where they came from, we don't know what their personal thoughts were, their loved ones, their families, but they went with the pride and dignity of being where they were and doing what they did, and even today their families share that.

If we do have to have another war, C. D. B. Bryan, for one, said he was glad to have men like Colonel Ripley on our side. David Winn, on the other hand, said he was glad that the country did not have to depend on the likes of himself. During the Vietnam War the army had declared him to be "psychologically unfit for military service." At the time he thought it was just a dodge to discharge him for his antiwar views. But, on reflection, he realized the army was right—he is psychologically unfit. His problem is (as is the problem of the characters in his novel *Gangland*) that he doesn't want to have enemies and that he can't cope in an environment where he has to have enemies. Since enemies are a part of the human landscape, he can't cope. And since everyone had too many enemies in the 1960s, the country has an aversion for enemies right now, and "America's soul is split." Yet, he agrees, "Colonel Ripley is right, we will have another war, but at least we are developing a literature to deal with it."

If Laos or Vietnam are any example, Asa Baber warned, the next war will come very quietly, whether or not our soul is healed.

Essay The Crybaby Veterans

If Vietnam came quietly, it has yet to become a quiet memory. Ron Kovic's outbursts remind us how deep the hurts of the Vietnam War still are and how quickly the shrill voices of the '60s can invade our thoughts and feelings. Colonel Ripley's recalling of MacArthur's tribute to the fallen of World War II and of Korea seemed to have been fitting enough for the survivors of these two conflicts. They were able to bury their comrades, and their memories, and take up the task of reintegrating themselves into the mainstream of American life. As Sloan Wilson described in his novel *The Man in the Gray Flannel Suit* (1955), it wasn't always easy, but these veterans raised no public outcry—of course, it helped that no one from society rose to denounce them—and confined whatever outbursts they may have had to their own homes. Not so Vietnam veterans. If Ron Kovic is any kind of representative of this group (and there are certainly those who would dispute this), MacArthur's words do not offer much balm. The memories, for many, are still recurring nightmares. And some, in their unvented passions, persist in thrashing about like blinded Samsons.

Thus the contemplation of the literature on the Vietnam War is far from a mere academic exercise. People still hurt. American society remains irresolute. And the future presses, with its taunts of, and beckoning to, a menu of next wars (Nicaragua, Libya, Afghanistan) for tomorrow's veterans. A society, though, need not be totally helpless in submitting to its next war. It can say, "No." It can say, "Yes." It can say, "Only under these conditions with this strategy and moral limits." But it can say none of these things coherently if the memory of the last war rings too discordantly in its ears.

These thoughts, basically in response to James Webb's speech and Ron Kovic's outbursts, prompted in my mind a personal vignette and a series of questions.

John Armistead is a friend of mine. In fact, he is the godfather of my son Scotty, who is five. John is a veteran of both World War II and the Korean War and lives across the street from my in-laws. Daymond Turner, my father-in-law, is a veteran of World War II. Both Daymond and John have sons, but they came of age in the 1970s and elected not to participate in the all-volunteer forces of the United States military. Horace Reeves is another friend who lives across the street. Horace also is a veteran of World War II. His son Pete is of military age. Although Pete is duly registered for the draft at his nearest post office, he is not planning on entering the military anytime soon. I am a veteran of the Vietnam War, but I am not planning on becoming a soldier again—like John had to do in Korea.

Occasionally, John, Daymond, Horace, and I talk about our wars. Once, I was beginning to describe the anguish I felt during the Cambodian Incursion of 1970 when my unit was pulled from its regular training, put through a riot control course, and ordered on alert for possible deployment against demonstrators on Washington, D.C.'s Ellipse. Before I could finish, John interrupted with what was nearly a curse, "Vietnam veterans are crybaby veterans." This is not precisely how this remark happened, but artists, we have been told, are entitled, in pursuit of greater and more transcendent truths, to play around with the facts a little. In any case, even though I knew John didn't mean it personally, it was hard for me not be a bit miffed. But, after all, I reflected, John had a certain right to his outburst. In the phrase used throughout the conference, he had been in "heavy combat" in both World War II and in Korea. Much like Tom Rath, I think, in Sloan Wilson's novel, he had quietly rejoined American society. But he, too, had "lost his place in line" and was not welcomed home by any parades or yellow ribbons.

Further reflection on his remark—and on those of James Webb, Ron Kovic, and Al Santoli—has made me wonder about all the stridency over Vietnam. What really was so terrible about the war that it arouses such rabid emotions? Many of today's college students spent the entire Tet Offensive in diapers, and whenever they come to the occasional campus debate on Vietnam among my fellow colleagues and hear it turn so quickly venomous, they look at us as if we have a touch of madness. Maybe we do.

Why do we think Vietnam was a uniquely evil war? Was it the means used? Despite Cornell University's study of gross bombing tonnage dropped in Vietnam as exceeding by many times over the tonnage dropped in all of America's previous wars, the actual physical damage was far less than that inflicted on Germany or Japan in World War II or on the American South during the Civil War. For all the talk of napalm and the searing image of Kim Phuc running naked down Highway 13 near An Loc from a misdirected strike of the "white fire," civilian casualties were much lower in Vietnam, both absolutely and proportionately, than in World War I, World War II, or Korea. In Korea, as Guenter Lewy (1978) has pointed out, every major city was left in ruins, and perhaps three million civilians lost their lives. This figure, incidentally, is greater than *all* deaths suffered in Indochina during both the French and the American phases of the war.

Was it the end, or a dubious cause, for which the war was fought? Vietnam, however, was not the first dubious war for the United States. The Mexican-American War (1846–48) was not the most moral of interventions. Aspects of our Indian Wars were "unspeakably evil." Our various ill-starred attempts to conquer Canada displayed thinly disguised venality and opportunism. The Spanish-American War (1898–1900) was hardly an exercise in unvarnished altruism. Even the "limited war" in Korea stirred up its ambiguities. Nor is Vietnam the first time we have looked foolish. General John Pershing only partly redeemed himself in World War I after his fruitless pursuit of Pancho Villa throughout northern Mexico in 1916.

So why was it so terrible? Was it something unique about Vietnam? Or was it that the sensitive generation of the '60s had had so much consciousness-raising about the horrors of warfare that they would have turned against any war, and Vietnam happened to be the only war lying around at the time? Would the flower children of the '60s have spurned the crusade against fascism in the 1940s? If Ron Kovic had been "raped" at Anzio instead of near the Ashau Valley, would he have called Roosevelt a Hitler, too?

I can imagine a novel set around my father-in-law's living room. We, the characters and veterans of three American wars, are discussing the merits of military service in Central America. Pete is listening in tortured anguish and Scotty is unconcernedly playing with his He-Man figures on the floor. The novel could go one of several ways and be equally authentic. Pete could go off to Canada and eventually persuade Scotty to join him as the war dragged on. Or Pete could develop a case of patriotism and go join the fight, with Scotty following eventually if Pete and his cohorts cannot resolve the war in time.

So the legacy of Vietnam remains ambiguous with both artistic and societal resolution still in the mist. My fear is that the mist won't clear until we have another war, and we see what happens to Pete—and to Scotty.

3 Down the Slippery Slope

Tensions Between Fact and Fiction

The difference between fairy tales and war stories is that fairy tales begin with "Once upon a time," while war stories begin with "Shit, I was there!"—*Lydia Fish, conference participant*

From the "heat" generated by Wednesday afternoon's debate, it became clear that "light" would be possible only if we could all get our "facts" straight. Getting them straight, and literature's responsibility in doing so, emerged as a central issue or problem of the conference. It is a problem because our facts are tangled up in our personal experiences. As Robert Oxnam said in his opening remarks, whether or not we actually served in Vietnam, those of us who were adults in the 1960s in America were involved in the Vietnam experience. We were all there. From this involvement, many of us have long since developed our perspectives and our commitments to our own set of facts about this war.

The literature, for one thing, has been quite voluminous, that is, persistent—and vivid. Even during its lean years, it has not let us forget the Vietnam War. What makes the hell of combat so poignant in these novels is that most of the principal characters, whom the authors take such care to create, all seem to get killed or maimed. James Webb, in his *Fields of Fire* (1978), and John Del Vecchio, in his *The 13th Valley* (1982), are like gods shattering their own creatures. More than just the unhappy endings, for the characters that are allowed to live, their lives slide down a slope of moral deterioration as inevitable as the degeneration of the soul in

Plato's *Republic*. It is tragic and somehow un-American—except that these tragedies as described by Philip Caputo, in *A Rumor of War* (1977), or by Winston Groom, in *Better Times Than These* (1978), happen to very convincingly American *boys* who become *men* in "moral reverse."

Frankly, it can all become too intense, both the memories of the war itself and much of the literature that has gushed from them. No wonder some of the novels have "tripped out" onto surreal planes. Occasionally these trips have been elevating in their playful whimsy and intrigue. In this vein, Tim O'Brien's *Going After Cacciato* (1975) and William Eastlake's *The Bamboo Bed* (1969) can almost be called delightful. More often, however, these journeys become downward spirals for the veterans into drugs and violence after returning from a war that stripped them of their moral gyroscopes. This more depressing route is at its most depressing in Robert Stone's *Dog Soldiers* (1973).

Despite the 130 novels already counted by John Clark Pratt in his bibliographic essay on the literature of the Vietnam War, all the conference participants agreed that *the* Vietnam novel has yet to be written. In depicting all these memories and in attempting to strike at the essence of the war itself, then, what should the literature and its authors strive to do? Should future writers stick to and reflect the facts, on the controversial supposition that the literature thus far has added to the distortion of the war rather than assisted in bringing about its clarification? But what are the facts? As Lawrence Lichty pointed out in his agenda paper, even official histories are based on a selection of some facts and not others. The real question that he asked of his panelists is: whether in fiction or in nonfiction, which facts of the past will be the remembered ones, or "historical facts," of the future? While some participants pondered the enormity of this question, and its responsibilities, Wallace Terry had no difficulty deciding which would quickly become the forgotten fact of the war: the Black Americans who fought there. Some, most notably Tim O'Brien and Stephen Wright, resisted Lichty's question entirely and contended that imagination was the writer's richest resource as he sought to weave a memorable story whose truth would be fictive and transcendent, unbound by any obligation to historical fact, whether past or future.

With these questions as their meat, Wednesday morning's (8 May) two panels on the "Literature on the War Experience" had a lot to chew on. In confronting what the literature should move on to, and what its responsibilities should be, the discussion wound its way through the vagaries of the publishing industry and an appreciation of the tremendous variety and range of experience that the war and its literature embodied. This sparked a remarkable controversy over the necessity of experience in writing good war literature. Such a debate quickly led to a brainstorming on how to write good literature, "literature that lasts." First, the participants considered the vital role of imagination, then weighed the merits of different forms of writing (fiction versus nonfiction, poetry, oral history), and finally tentatively tackled the question: what is good literature? In giving the general answer that it tells the truth, the group got tangled up in various views on how to tell the truth. These views brought everyone back to the original debate over fact versus fiction and a final consideration of the purpose of literature, and, again of what will last after the facts disappear.

Throughout the morning the conference steered well clear of any shoals that might have sparked another raging controversy. It was an earnest, if inevitably inconclusive, discussion that, for all its ambiguities and unresolved debates, was full of good advice, suggestions, and warnings for those writing on the Vietnam War. Again, I have taken the liberty to rearrange the "history" of the morning's panels to follow the path of these themes.

For the record, again, I would be remiss if I did not acknowledge the unscrambled historical "data base" to this account. In the first session the moderator, Lawrence Lichty of the University of Maryland, led three novelists through a discussion on the "Combat Literature" of the war: John Del Vecchio, *The 13th Valley* (1982); Jack Fuller, *Fragments* (1984); and William Pelfrey, *The Big V* (1972). Michael Stephens of Columbia University had his work cut out for him as moderator of the second panel. He steered two novelists (Tim O'Brien, *Going After Cacciato* [1975] and Stephen Wright, *Meditations in Green* [1983]), a poet (Bruce Weigl, *The Monkey Wars*, 1985), and an oral historian (Wallace Terry, *Bloods*, 1984) through a session on "Fact and Fiction in the Literature."

For all the 130 novels that have been written on Vietnam—and the spate of movies, TV shows, veterans' parades, and T-shirts that has come during the last two or three years—there was a long period when precious little was being published on Vietnam, either from the left or the right. Speaker after speaker rose to the conference floor to tell his story. Bruce Weigl's poems were rejected because the publisher was "no longer interested in the subject." Bill Ehrhart had to wait ten years for any of his poetry to be published. James Webb talked earlier of running through nine publishers. No one could top Wally Terry's list of 120 publishers as he struggled with the special problem of publishing not just an oral history on Vietnam, but one on the black experience in the war.

It seemed a relief to the entire conference when Jervis Jurjevics rose to admit that this was all true.

> **Jurjevics:** I worked in publishing for about sixteen years. . . . Last night I was very interested to note the paranoia on the part of the Vietnam veterans and authors of fiction, especially about their sense of having been rejected by the publishing community and submitting their material over and over. It was fascinating to note because the paranoia was really completely well-founded. I don't think anyone here in this room from publishing would ever deny it either. We sat for years in editorial boards and marketing meetings turning down novel after novel. . . . For a period of time well into the 1970s, the Vietnam novel was really an obscenity. . . . Ironically some of the ones turned down went on ten years later to win first novel awards.

Jurjevics went on to say, however, that to call this discrimination a conspiracy against the veteran is to ascribe too much strength to the publishing community. For all the industry's high idealism, it really follows the lead of the popular culture and serves as its litmus paper. Unfortunately, what turned the public around on Vietnam, and changed the attitude of publishers, was not a literary work but the success of a few films. *Apocalypse Now*, *The Deer Hunter*, and *Coming Home* come to mind in particular.

To Bill Pelfrey, this "confession" only underscored the validity of John Clark Pratt's insistence that each of the 130 novels in his essay has to be considered from two separate contexts: the time of the story itself and the time when the book was published. Pelfrey's book, *The Big V*, was called obscene by the *Library Journal* when it came out in 1972 and sold few copies even though it was nominated for the National Book Award. Had it been published later, it might have enjoyed a success similar to *Fields of Fire* and *The 13th Valley*, whose stories dealt with the same period but were published much later. All of the authors at the conference, however, including Pelfrey, made it clear that writers could not concern themselves with conforming to transient literary fashions and viewpoints. Ultimately, their stories will be heard.

Now that these stories are all coming out, what is truly remarkable about this literature is its diversity and tremendous range of experience. In his keynote address Jim Webb noted that "Vietnam was many things. It varied year by year, place by place, unit by unit." In fleshing out just how varied this experience of Vietnam was, John Del Vecchio tried to present a three-dimensional graphic representation of this diversity. On the x-axis he drew the time line of John Clark Pratt's seven-act play (including the prologue and epilogue) of the Vietnam War. On the y-axis he put down the seven topographical regions in which the Indochina war was fought. On these two axes alone, you get a grid of forty-nine possibilities. Adding a z-axis to incorporate a minimum of personal characteristics like age, rank, race, education, and military job, you can get as many as five hundred different experiences. No wonder the literature still lacks a unifying theme and remains fragmented.

Regarding all these experiences, a real division of opinion opened up as to whether this direct combat experience was necessary to write a good war novel. In his usual clarifying or at least crystallizing role, it was Bill Ehrhart who brought this issue sharply to the surface. Taking off on Bill Pelfrey's comment, "No one who has never been in combat can really understand that experience," Ehrhart threw out this challenge.

> **Ehrhart:** If that's true, why do you as writers about the combat experience bother to write about it? Who are you talking to? You're not telling me about combat [Bill is a marine combat veteran]. So if it cannot be explained to people who weren't there, who are you writing for, and why do you do it?

In response, Bill Pelfrey admitted that war novelists do not write for other combat veterans but really more for the historical record. Like the World War I literature, the Vietnam War literature provides the veteran his distinctive perspective in the larger context of his generation. The literature gives a record of the veteran's emotions, a record, Bill feels, that can come only through fiction.

John Del Vecchio's answer took a different tack. Although all novelists write to be entertaining, enlightenment is the primary goal of the writer, both self-enlightenment and public enlightenment. As he said, "much of the post-combat soldier's story is a story of a search for meaning." While personal experience itself might not be necessary, "For myself, I feel if you don't understand the history, if you don't understand the topography, and if you don't understand the cultural, political, and physical mechanics of what occurred; you will not be able to understand lasting meaning."

This grounding of fiction in personal experience and in history perturbed Jack Fuller.

> **Fuller:** As far as I'm concerned, it's time to stop thinking about the literature of the war as an appendix to the *Pentagon Papers*, as a set of documents to be judged by what they say about that particular time and that particular place. As long as we regard the books so narrowly, we invite others to consider them as artifacts rather than art. It is true that most of us started out to write about the war with an obsession to bear witness to extraordinary things we had seen, but if we did our work properly, I think it took us beyond our own experience. Writing fiction and poetry is . . . more than a means of recording something already discovered; it's a way of learning something we didn't know before. What we find out as we write is a different kind of truth than the things historians record in the books of days and hours. And if the writing is good enough, it transcends the passions, or the indifference, of the moment for the events that gave rise to our imagination about them.

In his agenda paper Tim O'Brien wrote, "At times, it seems to me, it is as if the writers are being held prisoner by the facts of their own Vietnam experiences. The result is a closure of the imagination, predictability and melodrama, a narrowness of theme, and an unwillingness to stretch the fictive possibilities."

I then asked the panelists if this was true: were their experiences more of a hindrance than a help to their creative writing?

For Bill Pelfrey, of course, the answer was "not at all." He "personally doubts that, despite Tolstoy's *War and Peace* and all of the other 'big canvas' books, anybody who hasn't experienced Vietnam can ever honestly capture it, whether the combat experience itself or the place of the veteran." John Del Vecchio agreed that we are imprisoned by our experience, but he also felt our experience could be built on to produce a "big canvas" book.

> **Del Vecchio:** I think we have a unique experience, but that doesn't mean we can't expand our experience into the political and cultural fields. I think that the more that we do that, the more that we understand, the deeper our own experiences and the deeper our own writings will be.

Jack Fuller, again, went a bit further.

> **Fuller:** Every writer runs the risk of getting trapped into an experi-
> ence in certain ways. . . . That's not only the danger, but also the
> strength and the resource that you draw on. Certainly, I think that if
> someone is writer enough, he or she could easily do a brilliant piece
> about Vietnam combat. Stephen Crane's experience of war at all post-
> dated his writing of *The Red Badge of Courage*. Henry James, I think,
> said, all it takes for a writer is that he be someone upon whom nothing
> is lost. It's not so much the distinctive personal experience, as some
> other vision. I think that's accessible to anybody.

Fred Downs may have put his finger more precisely on Fuller's "other
vision" by calling it "projection."

> **Downs:** Some of us have been in combat. Some of us have not been in
> combat. I don't think you have to experience the thing to be able to
> write about it. But you have to be able to project yourself into that
> person you are writing about. And once you've projected yourself into
> that person, you become that person.

He reminded the conference that this is the stage where the current
generation of Vietnam War writers find themselves: capturing the hell of
the combat experience. He admitted, though, that it may be time to move
on, for writers to grow into and learn about other aspects of the Vietnam
experience . . . and, I might add, to tackle things no longer traceable to
direct experience.

Whether from experience or not, Bill Broyles made the point that good
literature lasts. It lasts not from conforming with the popular mood at the
time but from reinventing the form of the experience in such a way that it
gives images and metaphors that will stand as an unforgettable memory of
the reality of the war. This is what Joseph Heller achieved for World War
II, Stephen Crane for the Civil War, and Erich Maria Remarque for World
War I. No one, he felt, had done this yet for Vietnam. How could it be
done?

Bill Pelfrey was not sure of the answer, but, he agreed, it could not be
done by trying to follow the fashion of the moment. Sounding a theme that
others picked up later, he said it would "have to depend on something
that's more honest." He went on to say that this would have to be "real
history, real literature, real poetry, and real drama."

This obviously raises the question, in answering Broyles's question of how it can be done: what is real, or at least how can we communicate it? To Stephen Wright, and to Tim O'Brien and Bruce Weigl, the key to communicating real literature lies in the imagination.

> **Wright:** I believe deep down that imagination is the very instrument of [this] reality. Finally, when you pursue this topic long enough, this whole thing of fact-fiction, it finally does blur to the point where imagination is just as real as a rock. For human beings I think in many ways it's more real than a rock. Because we live in our heads all of the time.

This is precisely the point that Tim O'Brien wanted to make.

> **O'Brien:** Now imagination, this act of imagination isn't "Hobbity" or "Alice in Wonderland." It's a real thing and I think influences in a major way the kind of real-life decisions we made, both to go to the war or not to go to the war. Either way, we imagine our futures and then try to step into our own imaginations. . . . For me, most of my service in Vietnam was spent in my head. I was aware of the things going on around me. I pulled the trigger when I had to and ducked most of the time. But I lived in my head a great deal.

Bruce Weigl, too, drew from his imagination for his poetry.

> **Weigl:** What the best of this work does, I believe, is to liberate us from facts and statistics and to provide us with a much broader and more human perspective on the war. Speaking personally, it was only through acts of imagination that I could finally find a form for my experience in the war.

If imagination, then, is the best resource for literature that lasts, what is its best form? Whatever the form, both Stephen Wright and Tim O'Brien felt that fiction is superior to nonfiction. Wright argued you can get a lot more out of an act of imagination than from nonfiction because in nonfiction all the data and raw facts impose inescapable patterns that you're not bound by in fiction. This is why, O'Brien claimed, he could take any truth or true story, however strange, and turn it into something weirder. Obviously, he would do this not just for the sake of making it weird, but for a larger dramatic purpose or truth.

In this connection, Bill Ehrhart rose to commend the special advantages of poetry as a form of imagination. A poem, he pointed out, can present a complete thought in a snapshot whereas historians, oral historians, and novelists have to trace their thoughts through full-length movies. To Bill, nothing illustrates this ability of a poem to produce a real truth, a kernel of human emotion, better than Bruce Weigl's poem, "Him, On the Bicycle," which Bruce, after some small show of reluctance, read:

In a liftship near Hue
the door gunner is in a trance.
He's that driver who falls
asleep at the wheel
between Pittsburgh and Cleveland
staring at the Ho Chi Minh Trail.

Flares fall,
where the river leaps
I go stiff.
I have to think, tropical.

The door gunner sees movement,
the pilot makes small circles,
four men running, carrying rifles,
one man on a bicycle
in the middle of the jungle,

he pulls me out of the ship,
there's firing far away,
I'm on the back of the bike
holding his hips.
It's hard pumping for two,
I hop off, push the bike.

I'm brushing past trees,
the man on the bike stops pumping,
he lifts his feet,
we don't waste a stroke,
his hat flies off,
I catch it behind my back
put it on, I want to live forever!

Like a blaze
streaming down the trail.

In a defense of nonfiction, both as a form of art and as a forum for truth, Wally Terry insisted that in his oral histories he tried to tell both good stories and true stories. Specifically he said, "I did all I could to incorporate into my approach the techniques of fiction writing. I want a character in each story who had to deal with moral issues. I want a story to have a good beginning, a good middle, and a good end. . . . Many of us have profited from the techniques of fiction." Indeed, one of the distinctive features of this highly varied body of literature on the Vietnam War is the number of first-rate oral histories that have been published by such writers as Michael Herr, Gloria Emerson, Al Santoli, Myra MacPherson, and, certainly, Wally Terry. They have proven to be an invaluable resource to those of us who are social scientists, historians, and journalists, and should provide good material for writers of fiction as well.

Whatever its form, good literature lasts, and, in general terms, it lasts, everyone agreed, because it tells the truth. What the truth is specifically, however, becomes quickly subject to the interpretation of politics, artistic expression, and morality. For James Webb, literature that tells the truth is literature that would be more reflective of the statistical profiles of his $6 million Veterans Administration study. It at least has a responsibility to be balanced, argued Colonel Ripley. Quite the opposite for James Chace, "Art is not propaganda. It tends to be a critique of the society, at least the best art does. In general, the artist is a subversive in the best sense of the word."

If art isn't government propaganda (or surveys), maybe it is anti-government propaganda (or truth). Perhaps this is unfair to C. D. B. Bryan, but these are his words.

> **Bryan:** It is our responsibility to make sure that those who lead us don't have the arrogance of those who led us through that period. We must, as Americans, celebrate what was best about America, which is us, the people, and not those men who led us and lied to us so badly. And not to let it happen again.

So how does one tell this unvarnished truth? Judging by the comments of some of the panelists, it seems to require a little lying. The problem for Stephen Wright is that, as an author, the factual material of the Vietnam War is so bizarre that many of the true stories, in fact, have a "tinny ring of inauthenticity to them," and to actually employ many of these factual coincidences and ironies in a book "would really, really ring false." Thus, in order to preserve the credibility of his own writing, "I just tried to stay away from too much of it."

Being somewhat less circumspect, Tim O'Brien came right out and said it, "Lying is a way one can get to a kind of truth." Tim meant this lying to be understood artistically. Fiction writers are not telling the entire, literal truth; they edit. They edit to dramatize the moral quandaries of life, and aim, not at "a definitive truth, but at a kind of circling...hoping that a kind of clarity emerges, not a truth." And, "issues can be clarified sometimes by telling lies."

While lying may serve an author's artistry, can it square with his moral responsibilities? Stephen Wright put it starkly when he said for the artist, "the only morality he has is never to lie." In fairness to Stephen, he did not mean that an author should never lie about facts, but that he should hold fast to his "honesty of vision," to be true to his "own perceptions of things, no matter how unpopular, how horrifying, how depressing and even seemingly how amoral they may be." These perceptions, he thinks, are the big benefit of literature. It opens up points of view and makes us aware of other lives. This is why we read it.

Based on human perceptions and moral vision, literature's truths, then, can be only partial at best. A writer's moral vision can encompass only what he can see, and, to Tim O'Brien, a writer sees, and indeed acts on, only what he can imagine. In this regard it was Wally Terry who pointed out that all "fiction was borne out of writing that originally was nonfiction." An author's imagination jumps off from what he has experienced or has come to know from other sources (historical knowledge, projections, and perhaps, revelations) to wrestle with Thoreau's dilemma of "How do you make a fact flower into a truth?" It is a process of selection that Stephen Wright described as moving from "crude fact to imaginative truth" by "making all these facts human and giving them human sense" through creative leaps of the imagination.

In this transition from crude fact to imaginative truth, we have come full circle to return to the fact-fiction dilemma. Do the imaginative truths of fiction provide us with new insights and better ways of understanding historical world events, like the Vietnam War? Or does a reliance on such free flights of imagination introduce such contradictions to the events that any reliance on these works for understanding—for truth—only results in distortion and mythmaking? Of course, in coming this full circle, we have also returned to the question of the responsibility of literature: does a good story have to be a true one?

If all that mattered was to tell a good story, then art could be for art's sake, and everyone could go home and write their fanciful hearts out, totally free of this pestering dilemma. No one at the conference seemed ready for such a glib surrender. Most held on to a sense of responsibility to a moral vision or to some kind of truth, even though this vision created ambiguities and confusion.

With these ambiguities, what is the basic reason for their writing, or to repeat Bill Ehrhart's earlier question: "Who are you writing for and why do you do it?" John Wheeler noted the reference by some of the panelists to "spiritual sickness" and "spiritual healing" and wondered if some writers used their literature to grapple with questions of faith and the quest for a transcendent truth to the war? Of the panelists only Wally Terry confessed to any kind of religious vocation to his writing. The rest ran away from the question, calling spiritual truth "mushy." As a source of inspiration, this gathering stood squarely in the modern age of secular humanism's partial truth. God, in this conference, no one admitted knowing. For Ron Kovic, Vietnam had killed God.

Despite this agnosticism in the conference's authors, their basic answer to Bill Ehrhart's question was that they wrote to tell the truth or at least some partial version of it, even if it was only their own individual "angle of vision," as Stephen Wright said. Arthur Egendorf rose to pose Bill's question about the purpose of writing more directly to this mission of truth-telling. He noted how often the word truth was used as "the great God-term," and yet in explanation it became bound up in such relativities as "angle of vision," "individual perception," and even "high-minded lying." If truth is so individual, why bother to write about it? In Arthur's words, "what kind of stories do you want to tell each other, to what end?"

Stephen Wright said that the basic purpose to his fiction is to "pose moral dilemmas." Tim O'Brien spoke in a similar vein: "For me, the purpose of writing fiction is to explore moral quandaries. The best fiction is almost always the fiction which has a character having to make a difficult moral choice." More specifically, Tim's concern is to probe the components of this choice, which, ironically, he finds to be a combination of fact and fiction: "What I'm interested in as a human being, not just as a novelist, is the interaction between memory and imagination, that is between fact and what we imagine. I think we operate as people, and in making moral choices, on the basis of those two big things."

To John Balaban it is this fundamental morality of literature that gives it its purpose. On behalf of this view, John cited Milan Kundera's assertion in his *Moral Fiction* that it is not the topic, subject, or politics of a fiction writer that gives him morality, but his ability "to teach us something we did not know before about ourselves."

Thus, if the truth of literature is relative, it is at least also additive, or, somewhat less mathematically, it is enlarging. With each new novel or poem, then, our understanding of the Vietnam War, and of the human condition more generally, should be expanding, circling and circling around a greater clarity of Vietnam's Truth. My only question of today's literary Sir Galahads, whom I admire very much, is: is this truth served by a pursuit only of moral quandaries and ambiguities? Some ambiguities can be dispelled by blending them in with some components of the obvious, or of new, "illumining facts." For example, when it was not clear who the Viet Cong were, their shadowy figures lurked menacingly, and very intriguingly, in the background of many a war novel. Now that we know a good deal more about the Viet Cong, and their organizations and institutional relationships are no longer in the shadows, are the Viet Cong, and the "truths" about them, no longer of literary interest because of a decline in their ambiguity? Perhaps dealing with the obvious makes for tinny, inauthentic reading. On the other hand, perhaps such added knowledge of our adversaries will allow for a novel on a larger canvas exploring the conduct of the war from both sides, and permit Tim O'Brien's truth-circling birds to spend a little time on the other side of the mountain.

This wanting to tell a good story but still not letting go of wanting to tell a true story at the same time, despite the artistic difficulties, moral compromises, and even rational contradictions involved, came home in Tim O'Brien's moving, vivid, and ambivalent summation:

> **O'Brien:** I'm a believer in the power of stories, whether they're true, or embellished, or exaggerated, or utterly made up. A good story has a power that I think Jack Fuller was trying to address, that transcends the question of factuality or actuality. Even though a fairy tale, "Hansel and Gretel" is a good story. *A Rumor of War,* being almost entirely true, is still a good story. . . .
>
> I think among the panelists there's a kind of unanimity in that with all of us, whether we write nonfiction, poetry, or fiction, we rely partly on fact and experience and partly on imagination. In writing nonfiction or fiction, we're aware that we're editing; we're aware that our subjects

are exaggerating, or that we may be exaggerating to get at a larger truth—like a fish story. You know the fish may seem really big when you're bringing that "mother" in, and to make that sense of bigness felt by the reader, you know the fish is getting bigger and bigger and bigger.

When one's writing fiction, in my case and in Stephen's case, we're making up grandiose cases, but we're after a kind of truth or clarity. I think the same is true with Bruce's poetry as well, that although in the poem he read, this guy wasn't sucked out of a helicopter—I mean he didn't witness this as a real event in the real world—it tells us something. It informs our souls or our spirits, and there's a kind of quickie feel to it.

Did Robert Frost ever really stop by that snowy woods, and where is that woods? Is it in New Hampshire or Vermont? What did it look like? Is it still there, and if it is still there, will it be there a hundred years from now? Five hundred years from now? Or will it be replaced by condominiums? And does it matter if there was a real woods or not? I don't think it does any more than it matters now to us whether there was a real Hamlet or a real Macbeth because the Hamlet or the Macbeth we have now is Shakespeare's Hamlet or Macbeth. And the Napoleonic Wars that we have with us now are, at least in my memory, those given to us by the writers.

I think that two hundred years, seven hundred years, a thousand years from now, when Vietnam is filled with condominiums and we're all going there to vacation on the beautiful beaches, the experience of Vietnam—all the facts—will be gone. Who knows, a thousand years from now the facts will disappear—bit by bit by bit—and all that we'll be left with are stories. To me, it doesn't really matter if they're true stories.

At this stage about the only definitive statement that can be made about the "Literature on the War Experience" is that it is pulling out of the dock of Lydia Fish's "Shit, I was there" war stories and is still some distance away from becoming "Once upon a time" fairy tales. As to Lawrence Lichty's original question to his panel: of all the possible stories, what is the story about Vietnam that *should* be told, or by which it should be remembered?, no one could answer.

Essay   What Are Facts?

If the participants of The Asia Society conference on "The Vietnam Experience in American Literature" had trouble in getting their facts straight (or even in deciding if it was important), they could take comfort in knowing that this problem extends to the U.S. Senate as well. In taking up the issue in the fall of 1983 of whether to grant President Reagan a resolution permitting the continued presence of U.S. Marines in Lebanon, senator after senator rose to invoke the memory of Vietnam—to justify opposite votes. Senator Charles Percy (R., Ill.) said he favored such an explicit resolution because he didn't want "to stumble into another Vietnam." Senator Joseph Biden (D., Del.), on the other hand, said he opposed the resolution because he didn't want the current generation "to suffer another Vietnam like my generation did." If The Asia Society conference has demonstrated a lack of artistic resolution to the Vietnam War, the Senate, and other national decision-making centers, continue to reveal the lack of a societal resolution. Mired in ambiguity, for all the "facts" that are pouring out on the war, the "real Vietnam" has still not been stood up where it can be seen.

Vietnam, of course, is not the only residue of ambiguity left over by history. Was Secretary of War Edwin Stanton behind the assassination of President Lincoln? Did the Russians really murder all those Polish cavalry officers in the Katyn Forest during World War II? In the postmortems on the Korean War, the motives for the original North Korean invasion are still unclear. Did Stalin order the attack, or did the Koreans do it on their own? As intriguing as these questions are, their resolution, one way or the other, no longer matters. People today, perhaps unwisely, are not drawing lessons from the Korean War.

But Vietnam is one residue that still does matter. People continue to draw lessons from it. Albeit in some confusion, Senators Percy, Biden, and others cast votes affecting many lives partly based on their views of Vietnam. To my way of thinking, an author may write a good story about Lincoln's assassination that is blatantly counterfactual to what is known because there will be very little social impact. The same is not true for the Vietnam War. If the commitment of the artists at the conference to some semblance of truth is genuine, then at least some regard for being true to the events of the war, if not to the facts themselves, strikes me as an important part of that responsibility.

This being said, the facts themselves are very difficult to ascertain. As in all historical events, some facts just plain disappear. Sometimes this neglect is relatively benign. Don Oberdorfer, in his *Tet!* (1971), immortalized the U.S. Marines in his account of their painstaking recapture of the imperial capital of Hue during the Tet Offensive, even as he completely ignored the feats of Army Air Cavalry units in clearing enemy forces from the hills around Hue. As Wally Terry pointed out, considerably more pernicious is the gradual lessening of the recognition played by blacks in Vietnam, a process fairly well completed for World War II with the recent publication of a special edition on that war in *Life* magazine without a single picture of a black. Wally predicted that a similar invisibility of blacks in Vietnam will be achieved by the year 2000.

What facts don't get forgotten often get twisted, to put it charitably. President Reagan has done much to champion the image of the Vietnam War as a "noble crusade." He revealed much of the basis for this memory in a news conference he held in April 1982:

> If I recall correctly, when France gave up Indochina as a colony, the leading nations of the world met in Geneva in regard to helping those colonies become independent nations. And since North and South Vietnam had been previous to colonization two separate countries, provisions were made that these two countries could by a vote of all their people together decide whether they wanted to be one country or not. . . .
>
> And there wasn't anything surreptitious about it, but when Ho Chi Minh refused to participate in such an election and there was provision that the peoples of both countries could cross the border and live in the other country if they wanted to, and when they began leaving by the thousands and thousands from North Vietnam to live in South Vietnam, Ho Chi Minh closed the border and again violated that part of the agreement. . . .
>
> And openly, our country sent military advisers there to help a country which had been a colony have such things as a national security force, an army if you might say, or a military, to defend itself. And they were doing this, I recall correctly, also in civilian clothes, no weapons, until they began being blown up where they lived, in walking down the street by people riding by on bicycles and throwing pipe bombs at them, and then they were permitted to carry side arms or wear uniforms. . .

But it was totally a program until John F. Kennedy, when these attacks and forays became so great, that John F. Kennedy authorized the sending in of a division of marines, that was the first move toward combat moves in Vietnam. . . . (cited by John Clark Pratt, *Vietnam Voices*, p. 3)

It is difficult to know where to begin in sorting out President Reagan's twisted memory. To begin with, although the history of Vietnam is a cycle of unity, fracture, and Chinese domination, prior to colonization Vietnam was one country under the Nguyen Dynasty. As for the elections, it was South Vietnamese President Ngo Dinh Diem who blocked them, not Ho Chi Minh. And it was Lyndon Johnson who sent the marines, not John F. Kennedy. One needn't belabor this, however, because Ronald Reagan has always been a man of vision rather than of history.

A man who should be in better command of his facts than Ronald Reagan is John Kenneth Galbraith, one of the war's most eloquent and effective critics. In his Phi Beta Kappa oration at Harvard University on 8 June 1982, he had this to say about the people of Indochina: "its calm and pleasant people have been returned to the peaceful obscurity for which nature intended them." If indeed obscurity is the preordained state of the Indochinese, until they were rudely interrupted by the American intervention, it is an obscurity that is hardly peaceful.

Errors like these of Reagan and Galbraith are easily correctable by an appeal to that part of the historical record that is free from controversy. But most of the facts of the Vietnam War are not so simple. Some of the most cherished interpretations of the war are being eroded by either the illumination of new facts or old facts that have changed. Daniel Ellsberg, for example, traced in his *Papers on the War* (1972) the path he took to reach the conclusion (or interpretation) that the war was a crime. I wonder if he would have stuck to this same path were he to walk it today? Ellsberg's first discomfort occurred when he realized that the Eisenhower administration supported South Vietnamese President Diem's refusal to hold national elections in 1956. While this is true, it is also true that Premier Chou En-lai of China put in his own fair share of effort in undermining the elections by his machinations at the 1954 Geneva Conference. In a study published just after Ellsberg's book, Jeffrey Race (*War Comes to Long An*, 1972) revealed through his publication of secret communist documents that the North Vietnamese never expected the elections to take place anyway.

While these revelations of Chou En-lai's machinations and the secret communist documents certainly do not absolve the U.S. government from its share of responsibility, they at least add some perspective that is lacking in Ellsberg's account.

From the thwarted 1956 elections, Ellsberg's soul-searching reached a judgment of criminality based on two conclusions. First, he concluded that the Viet Cong were largely indigenous southerners locked in a civil war with the Saigon regime. This immediately led him to the conclusion that the American bombing of North Vietnam was unjustified and demonstrated a criminal "arrogance of power." His first conclusion owed much to the writings of two Frenchmen, Jean Lacouture and Phillippe Devillers, whose book, *End of A War* (1959), argued this case persuasively. With respect to the bombing, evidently both Daniel Ellsberg and his boss Robert McNamara were deeply moved by Harrison Salisbury's eyewitness account of the destruction in the north, *Behind the Lines—Hanoi* (1967).

Subsequently, much has come to light that casts serious doubts on the bases for Daniel Ellsberg's judgment. For one thing, after the war official histories of the Indochinese Communist party made it clear that Hanoi directed the communist war effort from the start. Lacouture even made a trip to Vietnam in 1976 and returned to Paris publicly admitting he had been wrong about the Viet Cong. On the bombing, Ellsberg's moral horror may rest on more solid ground, but his assertion that "twelve megatons" of ordnance fell on Vietnam belies the fact that actual destruction and casualties were far less than what occurred in World War II or Korea.

Finally, the Americans were not the only ones whose power was arrogant. Truong Nhu Tang, a leading southerner in the Viet Cong infrastructure, wrote in his recent memoirs (1985) that with the Tet Offensive of 1968 all hope for an independent southern communist political force faded as northern domination became total. In his words, "the national democratic revolution itself became a casualty, choked by [an] arrogance of power" (p. 310). If nothing else, Tang's book makes clear that Americans have largely misread the meaning of the Tet Offensive.

My point in this exercise has not been to launch a vendetta against Mr. Ellsberg, but to use his case to illustrate how major interpretations of the war can be undermined by the shifting historical sands beneath them. An equally illustrative case could be made of a more conservative, or hawkish interpretation of the war. A cherished such view is that the Americans basically had the war won by the Christmas bombing of 1972. Alan Dawson eagerly points out in his book, *55 Days: The Fall of South Vietnam* (1977), that by the second week of the bombing the North Vietnamese had shot off all their surface-to-air missiles and stood defenseless before America's aerial armada. Their will was finally broken and they sued for peace. This line of conservative argument then contends that the communists went on in 1975 to snatch a victory from the jaws of this defeat through the paralysis of Watergate, congressional aid cutbacks to Saigon while Soviet support of Hanoi's war machine continued unabated, and the final blow of American inaction in the face of Hanoi's culminating 1975 offensive.

As in the case of Daniel Ellsberg, this victory myth is difficult to sustain in light of other facts and subsequent events. To begin with, the terms Hanoi received in the Paris Peace Agreement of January 1973 were hardly those of a defeated power. One hundred fifty thousand of their soldiers were allowed to remain in the south, while virtually all American troops had to be withdrawn in sixty days. Also, Hanoi's ability to mount another massive offensive in 1975, fight the Cambodians in 1977 and 1978, take on the Chinese in sharp border battles in 1979, and occupy and wage a campaign against Cambodian rebels throughout the '80s is a record that decisively refutes the suggestion that its will had been broken at Christmas of 1972. Even without Watergate and even with American reintervention, the struggle would have continued. Also, to focus on American actions in this period dangerously ignores the serious defects and blunders of the Thieu regime's final two years.

In following these two interpretations to their doom of error, with the facts of Vietnam in such a flux, perhaps some small measure of comfort can be taken in the certainty that eventually everyone will be wrong. The facts, in Vietnam, make liars of us all. Conversely, prominent lies can turn into profound truths, for the moment.

If the conference has set out the difficulties in making facts flower into truths in literature, in the social sciences, which are trying to do the same thing, how do you make a fact flower into a truth when the fact changes right in front of your eyes? An image that epitomized for many the brutality of the war was the summary execution of a Viet Cong cadre in a Saigon street by the Saigon police chief during the Tet Offensive. Seventeen years later we find out that that innocent Viet Cong had just murdered the police chief's best friend and entire family. In 1964 Congress gave President Johnson the Gulf of Tonkin Resolution that granted him the power to wage war in Southeast Asia in response to two attacks on U.S. destroyers by North Vietnamese PT boats. Now evidence in the recent Westmoreland-CBS libel trial has again come out that casts doubt on whether the second attack at least ever took place.

How do you make a fact flower into a truth when views about them can change so sharply? One man who took the fall of Saigon very hard was the last U.S. ambassador to Vietnam, Graham Martin. After the fall he went from one congressional committee to another villifying the antiwar movement for bringing down such a terrible defeat on the United States. In a telephone interview ten years later Martin told a reporter that the movement should be congratulated for "helping end an unhappy cause."

These continual contradictions of the facts and various interpretations of the war have led David Fromkin and James Chace to conclude, in a Spring 1985 article in *Foreign Affairs*, that there are no lessons to Vietnam. Their article runs through a series of candidate lessons from both the left and the right and finds enough facts to contradict them all.

Despite the factual impasse, there remain the Vietnam War's incredible ironies. Tim O'Brien's claim that he can make any fact weirder with his fiction notwithstanding, some of the facts of the Vietnam War can strain the imagination of anyone. James Harrison is right: who could have imagined that the French would be defeated at Dienbienphu in a 55-day campaign and the Saigon regime would fall twenty-one years later in a similar 55-day period, or that an American bombing campaign would reopen in 1965 with Soviet Premier Aleksey Kosygin on hand in Hanoi? Some issues like these may be coincidental, but others are anything but coincidental and are full of meaning. They jar us, force us to look at things in unexpected ways, and get us to learn things we didn't know before.

Consider two of these ironies. One of the dominant truths motivating all Western foreign policy is Munich. Munich, one recalls, was the site of a conference in 1938 at which British Prime Minister Neville Chamberlain thought he had achieved "peace in our time" with Nazi Germany by acquiescing to Hitler's seizure of Austria in that year and to the dismemberment of Czechoslovakia. It was futile. Hitler went on to slake his appetite for *lebensraum* (living room) with the invasion of Poland in September 1939 that triggered the start of World War II. The lesson—or truth—then, is never again. Never again should one's policy appease an aggressor, because eventually the aggressor's restraint will break; so nip it in the bud. The North Vietnamese foment an insurgency in the south, and off the

Americans go to prevent another Munich by plugging the new hole in the dike of containment. But, ironically, the Vietnamese, too, have their Munich. Only their Munich occurred at the Geneva Peace Conference of 1954 where the Chinese, French, and Russians cheated them out of the victory that was rightly theirs. Had they had this victory ratified in Geneva, of course, there never would have been an American war in Vietnam. As it was, the Vietnamese communists vowed, "Never again": never again would they let themselves get cheated at the bargaining table.

Another irony concerns the American commander, General William C. Westmoreland. Westmoreland, both during and after the war, came under persistent criticism for his military strategy with its manifestations of "search and destroy," "body count," and "cross-over point." It was Westmoreland's fear that South Vietnam was vulnerable to a conventional assault consisting of a single thrust across the Central Highlands to the coast combined with an assault across the demilitarized zone along the coast that would join up to roll south in a giant drive to Saigon. In the Tet Offensive the communists struck everywhere at once, counting on a political uprising that never materialized, and the blow dissipated. In the Easter Invasion of 1972 the communists struck at four different places, thereby failing to concentrate their forces, and compounded this mistake with a critical hesitation at the demilitarized zone, and the invasion was turned back. However, in the final 1975 campaign they followed Westmoreland's fears to a T. They never thanked Westmoreland for handing them their strategy on a platter.

What these ironies do is show us a way out of this factual impasse. We need not follow Fromkin and Chace's nihilistic path of naysaying all lessons through a game of factual tit for tat. Not all facts are arithmetically equal. Some facts are more important than others; some ironies more instructive. Just as fiction writers edit and select in telling the truth, so, too, must nonfiction writers weigh facts and information, and count some more important than others. Sorting it all out to some rendering of a truth requires several things: it takes an enormous mastery of all sources of information so that a writer has the breadth to grasp the obvious and the depth to sense the ironies, and from the obvious and the ironic to make those creative leaps of the imagination that strike home at the thing's very soul.

Writers of nonfiction like myself can point out the obvious and highlight the ironies. But those leaps of imagination, I am the first to concede, come best from fiction. Fiction reveals emotions and can examine motives. It is in laying bare motives that we find out why things happen. And these are the real facts: the information that is put in an insightful pattern that allows us to understand.

An understanding of the Vietnam War is not going to come from one writer's personal experience alone. It is going to come from writing that will be able to make the experiences of others and their writings his own. He will have to incorporate facts that are not his own and that he has not known before. To make his pattern true, other facts, both fictional and nonfictional, are going to have to be related to his own, including the great lost fact of the Vietnam War literature so far, the Vietnamese people over whose hearts and minds the war was supposedly fought.

4 The Great Lost Fact

The Asians

I don't trust a man till I got his pecker in my pocket. — *President Lyndon Baines Johnson*

The wise man shuts his mouth,
The strong man folds his arms — *Vietnamese proverb*

Mahatma Gandhi, on Western civilization: I think it would be a good idea.

Throughout the conference many expressed discomfort over the lack of an Asian dimension to the literature on the Vietnam War. In his keynote address James Webb decried this shortcoming and said, further, that we have not served our Asian friends well by what we have written thus far. Bill Broyles, in trying to explain the problem, lamented that the Asian experience is "closed to us." Bill Pelfrey, despite his astute observations of the different types of Vietnamese he met in Vietnam, admitted he had trouble getting beyond the "numb stare" that seemed to be the GI's nearly universal impression of the Vietnamese. Thus, he wasn't sure if an American novelist could do any better than make cardboard personalities out of his Vietnamese characters. John Clark Pratt said he wouldn't even try to develop Vietnamese characters in his writing. Nevertheless, his *The Laotian Fragments* (1974) does a creditable job of portraying some Laotians, including the romantic (if arthritic) Hmong hill tribe commander, General Vang Pao.

If most of the literature on the Vietnam War is an exercise in American cultural narcissism, it only reflects the way in which Americans conducted the war itself. For journalists, the only events worth reporting were American actions. In the Easter Invasion of 1972, for example, with virtually all the American ground combat troops withdrawn, it was the American air strikes that got all the attention, even though South Vietnamese soldiers on the ground played a critical role in turning the North Vietnamese invasion back. Almost to a man and woman, none of these journalists knew Vietnamese. For the military, especially after the large units arrived, Vietnam was all "Indian country." Except for superficial and awkward episodes in the towns, the troops kept to themselves. They gave everything around them American names, and, when not on their intense patrols and sweeps, stayed in their bases drinking beer and watching movies. Equivalent patterns of cultural sheltering were erected in the rear areas. The major exceptions were for forays of whoring and, though seldom reported, for volunteer work in orphanages. Regarding the former recreation, Alexander Woodside reports in his *Community and Revolution in Modern Vietnam* (1976) that there were 300,000 prostitutes in Vietnam (p. 289). With 500,000 GI's this surely made for one of the most favorable soldier-to-courtesan ratios in the history of warfare.

I hasten to add, though, that this is not the aspect of the American experience in Vietnam upon which the conference dwelled. On Thursday morning (10 May), the last day of the conference, I chaired a session on the "Images of Asia and Asians in the Literature." For its panelists the conference was lucky to have three men whose sensitivity to Asia stood in sharp contrast to the general vacuum in the literature as a whole: Asa Baber, who wrote an early novel on Laos, *The Land of a Million Elephants* (1970), John Balaban, who has written several collections of poetry on Vietnam, most recently *Blue Mountain* (1982), and Al Santoli, who has come out with his second oral history, *To Bear Any Burden* (1985).

In recognizing (as the behavior of the conference participants only confirmed) that for Americans the Vietnam War still continues over here even as it has ended, or at least shifted ground, over in Indochina, I began the session with this entreaty:

> **Lomperis:** I don't think that we ever can approach the ending of this war for us until we can view it in a larger context. As authentic and as vivid and as powerful as the literature that has stemmed from these personal combat experiences is, we need to reach beyond ourselves. We started by comparing Vietnam to World War I and to

World War II. But we also need to remind ourselves most forcefully that this wasn't just an American war in which we can contemplate exclusively our own hang-ups and societal malaise. This war occurred in a country called Vietnam. It impacted as well on a culture and on a society that is Vietnamese. And until we bring these two highways (or experiences) together, we won't put either war to rest.

In working at bringing these highways together in the subsequent discussion, Asa Baber led off by contending that the greatest barrier to this task was American racism. Whatever the barriers, for John Balaban, coming to terms with the Asian reality of the war is crucial both politically for American foreign policy and culturally for a sense of who we are and who Asians are. No one was less hesitant in spelling out the terms of this Asian reality than Al Santoli. The sharp reaction to Santoli's historical treatise provoked the third and last lightning bolt of the conference. This bolt shot a ragged trajectory, with the main line of Santoli's exposition dented by the questioning of James Harrison, the author of a lengthy history of the war, *The Endless War* (1982), and jolted by the sharp attacks of Bill Ehrhart. With each of these interruptions, Santoli's vehemence intensified. Timely deflections by Arthur Egendorf and Tim O'Brien prevented this spiraling rhetoric from rending a very tattered fabric of civility. Arnold Isaacs's wry reminder that the Vietnamese never mattered to the Americans effectively closed the argument, and brought everyone around to a pessimistic harmony over such lamentable neglect. Again, to artistically trace the upward and downward path of these spirals, I have inflicted some damage on the actual sequence of the discussion. In the essay I will attempt to lighten the session's concluding pessimism by holding up the kind of insights on the war that can come from incorporating an Asian dimension into the literature.

Asa Baber began his point by recalling from my agenda paper that "people draw their lessons from their memories, from which set of images stay with them the longest." Images of Asians, then, are to Asa the heart of what the conference should be about. The struggle for political control is a struggle for the images in our heads. We draw our lessons from our images. We write our truths from our images. The core of Asa's point is that when we got involved in Vietnam our images of Asians were wrong. And they still are. They are racist, and they cannot be easily erased. But perhaps they can be overcome if their deficiencies are recognized.

For example, no one who saw on TV the Viet Cong cadre shot in Saigon can ever forget it, but the subsequent revelations of the event's circumstances can at least add some perspective to it, and, significantly, change somewhat one's image of the executioner. Initial repugnance, then, can be modified by subsequent sympathies.

Unfortunately, images usually work the other way. Newer images recall the darker sides of earlier ones, reincarnating dormant and ugly passions. Asa gave his own vivid example of this descent. The looming confrontation with Japan over trade in the 1980s, recalling similar tensions in the '30s well before Pearl Harbor, has given rise to a spate of mildly anti-Japanese cartoons in today's press. One that appeared in the *Chicago Tribune* on May 6, 1985, made Asa think back. It kindled something dark. The cartoon was of a Japanese family smugly content around their color TV set and other hi-tech Tinkertoys, wondering whether they should "buy American." The son looked like a Martian with buckteeth, wire-rimmed glasses, and a long, skinny neck. What flashed back into Asa's mind from the cartoon image of this kid's neck was the classic World War II photo of a naked-to-the-waist but dignified Australian officer kneeling before his captor and baring his neck before the upraised samurai sword of a particularly sinister-looking Japanese soldier. Images of fierce competitors provoke memories of vicious barbarians.

As a result, Asa found, "The way I've experienced the Asian Syndrome is that people just don't want to see Asians." This was brought home to him by the treatment meted out to his novel, *The Land of a Million Elephants*. Published in 1970, it was never reviewed. After a period of paranoia, Asa finally figured out what his problem was when people told him, "Gee, don't you understand, you can't get rid of your hero till the last page." They were talking, of course, about a white guy who died a quarter of the way into the book. But he was not Asa's hero. His hero was Buon Kong, an old Asian wise man. But as Asa said, people "couldn't relate to that"—an Asian hero.

Asa ended his point with an exhortation:

> **Baber:** What I'm saying is that I think we're all racists and we have to struggle to get over it. . . . We have to go to more than the literature of the novelists and poets on this side of the Pacific, on this side of the culture. We have to go to some of the nonfiction and read everything we can. Lady Borton, who is in this room, has written a book called *Sensing the Enemy* (1985). She has lived and nursed and worked with

Vietnamese refugees, and her firsthand knowledge and experience is helpful. . . . I'd like us to admit this racism and then just move on. And if we can, maybe we won't go to war so much. Maybe we'll try to work with people who we really think are our equals, rather than just people who are convenient strategically or tactically, and who we want to use for our own purposes.

That we have abused Asians like this in the past comes out most starkly in a set of percentages that are frequently excavated from the *Pentagon Papers*, most recently by Arnold Isaacs in his *Without Honor* (1983). John McNaughton, one of Defense Secretary McNamara's chief "whiz kid" lieutenants, put U.S. war aims in these terms:

> 70%—to avoid a humiliating U.S. defeat
> 20%—to keep Indochina from Chinese hands
> 10%—to permit the people of South Vietnam to enjoy a better, freer way of life. (p. 496)

One poet on this side of the Pacific who has drunk deeply of the culture on the other side is John Balaban. I think it is fair to say that he has overcome his racism. John, too, felt it was important to come to terms with Asia, and he brought slices of Vietnamese culture to the conference with a special beauty in the form of both the Vietnamese poems he spoke in English and the ones he sang in Vietnamese. Although studying Vietnamese culture has its own intrinsic reward, literature's attention to this culture can help the United States understand the war and thereby regain its sense of mission and how to carry it out. When John Clark Pratt said, "Literature is the best way to come to terms with Vietnam," he was operating from an implicit assumption that it *is* important to come to terms with Vietnam. John Balaban made the importance of Pratt's assumption quite explicit.

> **Balaban:** It is important for all sorts of reasons. The main one is that if we don't, if we try to forget about Vietnam, this country will become like a person who has suffered amnesia. The sky looks o.k. It doesn't fall down. He holds his drink in his hand and generally talks like everyone else. But there is something missing in his behavior that he can't quite account for, and that is a crippling disability. If we carry that disability of failing to understand Vietnam into the next century, then we are going to be a very weakened country indeed.
>
> This is a great country. We obviously have large worldwide interests,

and Vietnam has staggered our sense of mission. . . . It seems to me that this country has reached a point of empire where it is absolutely crucial for it to understand what other people think. . . . Literature, I think, can address that. . . . [In this regard] as writers we can do something valuable that is also political.

Balaban spelled out this political value to literature in two trenchant areas. First, it can help us overcome our narcissism; this is something, though, it still hasn't done.

Balaban: It isn't just that we lost that war, but it is also that they won it. It seems to me that a lot of our fiction talks about Vietnam as if it were something that went wrong in Alabama . . . something that we just couldn't figure out. We ought to know what happened in Vietnam, if only for patriotic reasons, especially when we are concerned about possible analogues between Vietnam and Central America. To understand the Vietnam War more fully, with greater instruction, we have to understand the Vietnamese.

Second, in terms of the ominous contests over images discussed by Asa Baber, literature can deflate, question, and humanize the stereotypical and inflammatory images of political rhetoric. This possibility gave John Balaban a sense of mission to his task of gathering the oral poetry of the Vietnamese in 1972.

Balaban: I had a very missionary sense of what I was doing. Saving the poetry might have something to do with saving these people. One thing that literature does is to make people believable. Rhetoric never does that. Rhetoric makes people killable. Fiction, poetry, and plays make everybody alive. They stay the hand that would pull the trigger, or would do those quiet things that start wars and teach us to disregard others.

On an individual level, Balaban has done much to dispel the opaque (and threatening) "mystique of the Orient" image through the compelling ordinariness of the Vietnamese peasantry that shines through both his poems and the sung poems he has compiled of the peasants themselves. In Vietnamese, John sung one about perfectly understandable tears shed over being left behind:

Love Lament

Stepping into the field, sadness fills my deep heart.
Bundling rice sheaves, tears dart in two streaks.
Who made me miss the ferry's leaving?
Who made this shallow creek that parts both sides?

(From John Balaban, *Ca Dao Vietnam: A Bilingual Anthology of Vietnamese Folk Poetry* [Greensboro, N.C.: Unicorn Press, 1980], p. 31.)

On a national or cultural level, underlying the technical virtuosity of these poems "is a body of philosophical belief that is interesting to listen to, if you want to know who these people are." What comes out, Balaban pointed out, are ideas and attitudes toward concepts that, when compared to Western approaches to them, can tell much of why the Vietnam War was intractable and difficult—and can make it clear that it was intractable and difficult precisely because it took place in Vietnam and not in Alabama.

Take power. Our Western concept of power is direct and arm-wrenching, with images of instant, ostentatious, and overwhelming force. LBJ was operating squarely within this tradition when he gloated, "I don't trust a man till I got his pecker in my pocket!" So also was General Curtis Le May when he suggested, "Let's bomb them [the North Vietnamese] into the stone age!" Arrayed against this style of Western macho was an Asian and Vietnamese conception of power that glorified in the indirect and the subtle, while remaining firm and capable of sudden acts of explosive force. This concept is expressed in the verbal brush strokes of the many Vietnamese proverbs that have such a strange pith to Westerners, such as:

"The wise man shuts his mouth,
The strong man folds his arms."

These proverbs go back to the stratagems of Sun Tzu, a contemporary of Confucius, and have come out today in the bedeviling strategy of people's war.

Certainly Western civilization cannot be indicted as a whole on the strength of some of its more brutal conceptions of power. There are, surely, without having to present a long list, some compensations that have developed over the years. But it is equally certain that in the recent colonial past, Asians have experienced enough of an overdose of these more brutal applications of Western civilization to make men like Gandhi wonder about it. If the careers of Mao Tse-tung, Ho Chi Minh, and Pol Pot—and the movements that have sprung from them—have exhibited their own out-bursts of vicious violence, it is because, in their Western Marxism and national xenophobia, they have combined the worst of both worlds.

Lightning Bolt III   The History Lesson

While many writers of the Vietnam War have used their pens to criticize the American conduct of the war and a few have sought to inject some Asian presence into this literature, Al Santoli, for one, has chosen to focus on the deficiencies of the Vietnamese communists. That he has done so in such unambiguous detail provoked a sharp reaction. In his attempt to provide the conference with some sketches of a history lesson on the war, Santoli faced a very unruly classroom. What follows is an account of his turbulent seminar.

Santoli began by relating his experiences with two wars in Indochina. In the first, the American phase, he served with a unit in 1968–69 that operated along the Cambodian border athwart a major infiltration route of North Vietnamese regulars, specifically the 271st Regiment. There he found that all the local people really wanted was to be left alone. Santoli then said that he firmly believed that if the North Vietnamese had not come, neither would the Americans, and the villagers could have had their peace. But it was not to be. Instead the 271st Regiment killed villagers for not informing it of the location of Santoli's unit.

Since then, in 1979, Santoli met one of these soldiers in Switzerland who had been trying to kill him in Vietnam. The man had defected because he could not stomach the Stalinist police state that was being constructed in Vietnam. Thus, for Mr. Santoli, "Communism, whether it be Chinese-inspired communism or Soviet-inspired communism, does not go along with the nature of people who want to be free. . . . In this regard, I will always feel that my involvement in Southeast Asia was the proper thing to do."

So, quite literally, Al Santoli returned to Southeast Asia to do it again. In 1983, after returning to Southeast Asia and interviewing such Cambodians as Prince Sihanouk and Prime Minister Son Sann as well as Vietnamese fighting the occupation of Cambodia by socialist Vietnam, he was again shot at by Vietnamese troops. They were soldiers of the same 271st Regiment, this time firing indiscriminately on a refugee camp of Vietnamese inside Cambodia. "Things," said Santoli, "haven't changed too much in Southeast Asia." In the literature, though, there has been very little recognition of this continuing slaughter and repression. "For some of us there that truly cared about the Vietnamese, for those of us who truly care still about the Vietnamese and Cambodians," he insisted that there needs to be an incorporation of this perspective into a broader understanding of the war. Interestingly, like Asa Baber and John Balaban, Santoli also called for more reading of Asian dimensions to the war, particularly of recent works by Vietnamese émigrés. However, like one man's fact being another man's fiction, Baber's, Balaban's, and Santoli's reading lists were quite different.

One historian who was not on Al Santoli's list was James Harrison. During the discussion period, Harrison contended that the feature of the Vietnamese communists that stands out above the march of historical events is their fanaticism. He pointed out that of the forty-two members of the top communist leadership in 1945, thirteen had been killed by the French and the rest had spent a total of 222 years in jail, which comes out to over seven years a man. When you have this kind of revolutionary situation, it seemed to Harrison, in light of what happened to both the French and the Americans subsequently, the lesson is clear: you stay out of the way and let the people evolve, in time, more reasonable policies and politics. And this to him is the central question to ask of Central America: is there a similar situation of revolutionary fanaticism?

In response, Santoli gave his presentation of Vietnamese history. His words ricocheted around the room, sending the conference into a confusing roller coaster ride of truth, bombast, rhetoric, and anguish.

Santoli: The only thing that I'd like to say is that a lot of the history that Americans have read of Vietnam either came from the French or from people sympathetic to Ho Chi Minh. What I've tried to do in *To Bear Any Burden* is to talk to a number of Vietnamese who have survived and were involved in other nationalist groups before 1945. For instance, the Yen Bay Mutiny (1930), which was seen as the first modern strike against the French, was not done by Ho Chi Minh's people, but by the VNODD [a nationalist party similar to the KMT in China]. There were a number of other nationalist parties involved in Vietnam. In southern Vietnam the largest communist party was not the Stalinist communists of Ho Chi Minh, but the Trotskyites, whose leadership was killed off by Ho Chi Minh's Stalinists. There were a number of other groups. There was the Advance Guard Youth which was largely non-communist, but willing to fight with anybody. Its leadership was killed off. The Dai Viet's leadership was killed off. The VNODD's was killed off. One of the great nationalists of Vietnam until the time he was killed off by Ho Chi Minh's people was President Diem's brother. Diem came to power after his brother was killed, and he went into exile because Ho had him arrested and attempted to coerce him into being a figurehead in his government. In knocking off all the other leadership, in effect Ho was trying to create a coup. One of the reasons the Americans went in there was to prevent this: what is happening now inside Vietnam. . . . I suggest that you at least have the open mind to look at other Vietnamese history and you'll see something quite different from what people who have supported the communist takeover have been propagating.

Harrison: I just want one final sentence. I completely agree that I would not like to see those fanatics in power, but how can you simply talk about who the Stalinists of Vietnam kill without also looking at who was killing first, or at least at the same time?

Ehrhart: If you would excuse me, I would just like to say to Mr. Santoli that I wish you wouldn't suggest that if I and others here were as smart and as knowledgeable as you, we would think like you. To hear you suggesting to Mr. Harrison, a professional historian who has written a very kind book on the history of Vietnam, that if only he knew the history, he would think like you, is a remarkable arrogance.

Santoli: Well, I don't think it is arrogance, since I've spent much of the past fourteen years with a hell of a lot of Vietnamese and Cambodians. And what I reflect is basically there. And also if you look at the fact that in 1968 during the Tet Offensive, when the Vietnamese had the opportunity to rise up against the government, they didn't. In 1972 during the spring offensive when the Americans were mostly gone, there wasn't a massive insurrection. In 1975, when the North Vietnamese stormed in, there wasn't any popular support.

Ehrhart: YOU ARE NOT THE ONLY ONE THAT KNOWS THIS, SIR!

Santoli: BUT I AM ONE OF THE FEW PEOPLE WHO DOES, SINCE THE PUBLISHING INDUSTRY HAS MOSTLY KEPT

THIS POINT OF VIEW OUT, AND ONLY PUBLISHED BOOKS
FOR THE MOST PART THAT ADVOCATED THE HO CHI
MINH POINT OF VIEW. IT IS VERY DIFFICULT WHEN SOME-
BODY LIKE MYSELF DOES MAKE THIS POINT, YOU ALL
GET UP IN ARMS. SO I DON'T THINK IT IS ARROGANCE
ON MY PART. IT ISN'T FOR ONE WHO HAS BEEN WITH
CAMBODIANS BEING SLAUGHTERED IN THE PAST TWO
OR THREE YEARS, WHEN MOST OF YOU HAVE SAT BACK
HERE AND DONE NOTHING ABOUT IT!

With this, the ride turned its last corner and people's stomachs began
to settle back from behind their lungs and other unseemly hiding places.
Arthur Egendorf was the first to recover with a still somewhat dazed
observation, "I am surprised that in a conference on literature talk of Asia
is so concrete." What surprised Tim O'Brien was that all this concrete talk
was still so unresolved. He jabbed the conference with a flurry of questions
that no one could answer and ensured that there would be no more turns to
the ride.

> **O'Brien:** Wouldn't all of us admit that a mistake was made in Vietnam?
> There was a great uncertainty and ambiguity and ignorance about
> what the Vietnamese wanted and what the culture was. Does it seem
> to you that a nation should commit an armed war—killing lots of
> people—for uncertain reasons? And even if Mr. Santoli is right in his
> argument that we misunderstood Vietnamese history, in a way it doesn't
> matter, does it? Because no one knew anything back then, and we
> were shooting anyway. And if now fifteen years later there is still this
> vast division in this room, ought not a nation raise these questions
> prior to going to war than go to war and then ask questions?

It remained for Arnold Isaacs to bring the ride to a complete stop. He
started by observing, "If this conference has made nothing else clear, it has
certainly made it clear that it is not yet possible to separate the art and the
politics of the war." In looking at the political history of the American
involvement in Vietnam since the 1940s, "it suddenly dawned on me that
from beginning to end, American policy was never determined by any
consideration of Vietnamese realities anyway." In the French phase our
concern was over what was happening in Europe. Our need there was to
make the French a valuable ally, so we supported them in Vietnam. Echo-

ing John Balaban's earlier contention, Isaacs pointed out that what was happening in Vietnam could have been happening in Uganda, or Venezuela, or Samoa; our policies would have worked out about the same. In the 1960s when we decided on our intervention, again we weren't looking at Vietnam. Instead, there was a simple assumption that Vietnamese communism was an extension of Chinese communism, which was equivalent to the Nazis spreading across Asia, and it had to be contained. After our rapprochement with China in 1972, staying on in Vietnam (brief as it was from that point) became a matter of preserving our credibility. Inseparably, the literature seems to have followed this same sorry path. Thus, Isaacs's conclusion is doubly damning:

> **Isaacs:** The Vietnamese are absent from the history of American policy formation, just as much as they are absent from most of these novels. They were in the scenery, but they were not anything that we were really looking at. And this is a big part of why the effort turned out to be so costly and so unsuccessful.

On this, Asa Baber, John Balaban, and Al Santoli were in complete agreement. In achieving consensus from such disparate quarters around a rallying cry of "Never again"—never again should Americans in Asia ignore the realities and culture of the world's vastest continent—a central purpose of the conference may have been fulfilled.

Essay   Reading the Asian Wind

To return to Asa Baber's concern for the political and literary struggle over images, and the lessons that are drawn from them, when asked what are the dominant images of Asians that appear in the literature, the answer is simple. The images of Asians presented in the literature are so muted that there really are no dominant images. Thus if any misperceptions of the Vietnamese have grown out of the literature, they have come most fundamentally from the literature's very lack of perceptions of the Vietnamese. In the literature to date, they are either simple and childlike or devious and treacherous, which is to say mysterious—which is to say nothing. Michael Herr summed up the problem in getting beyond these glib characterizations when he lamented, in his *Dispatches* (1978), that reading the faces of the Vietnamese "was like trying to read the wind." Hence, the lesson that can be drawn from our understanding of Asia through our political experience and literature on the Vietnam War is that we don't have a good enough understanding yet to draw any lessons.

In fairness to the literature, however, Asia and Asians have certainly not been ignored altogether. To borrow Michael Herr's image of the literature, many works do provide "illumination rounds," or "fragments," as John Clark Pratt would have it. Before going on to discuss how American writers might penetrate the "numb stare" and read between the lines of this Asian wind, I think it is worthwhile to pause briefly to see where we are, and take a look at a few of these rounds.

In the combat literature James Webb's *Fields of Fire*, amid all the carnage, does contain a good picture of the effects of a marine sweep through some villages from a Vietnamese perspective as well as a superb portrayal of the motives behind a Viet Cong rallier to the U.S. Marines. David Halberstam's, *One Very Hot Day* (1968), written about the earlier Adviser Phase of the war, does provide some insights into the personalities of two Vietnamese army officers. In fact, they get equal billing with their American counterparts. In addition, Halberstam's portrayal of the heat of the Delta will prompt any Vietnam vet to reach for a canteen. Tim O'Brien offers equally evocative descriptions of the Vietnamese countryside in *Going After Cacciato*. In fact, the hero, an Iowa farm boy, establishes a special affinity with this ancestor-worshipping land. O'Brien even digs underground and unearths a hopelessly lost and "spaced-out" North Vietnamese "tunnel rat."

Some of the more political works also make attempts at integrating the Vietnamese and their culture into their stories, not always with great success. The first *American* novel that brought Vietnam to the attention of the American public was William Lederer and Eugene Burdick's *The Ugly American* (1958). Their mission was to demonstrate the application of Maoist theory to Asian poverty, and the glaring incompetence and ignorance of the American foreign policy establishment in failing to come to grips with it. Perhaps provocative at the time; today it sounds too didactic. Two novels about ambassadors also try to build an Asian presence into their Vietnamese setting. Morris West's *The Ambassador* (1965) is all about the assassination of President Diem and the Buddhist Crisis in 1963. The theme, of course, is that the ambassador fails to avert a tragedy by his inability to master the subtleties of Buddhist metaphysics. The book begins and concludes with an essay on Zen dialogue that leaves us all in even worse shape than the hapless ambassador. The mystery of the Orient overwhelms and blinds us Occidentals again. Less philosophical by the end of the war, Bernard Kalb and Marvin Kalb's *The Last Ambassador* (1981), in recounting South Vietnam's last fifty-five days, does take time to consider the human plight of the Vietnamese, but most of the book is busy trying to get the ambassador and his entourage out of the country before they are overwhelmed by North Vietnamese tanks.

More than "illumination rounds," some works do have a substantial Asian content. Besides the writings of Asa Baber, John Balaban, and Al Santoli, prominent among these are Robert Olen Butler's *The Alleys of Eden* (1981), Charles McCarry's *The Tears of Autumn* (1974), Charles Collingwood's *The Defector* (1970), Loyd Little's *The Parthian Shot* (1973), and Donald McQuinn's *Targets* (1980). The problem with even these novels is that too often despite their Asian content, they essentially use this content more for dramatic purposes than to really convey insights into the Asian dimensions of the war. The mildest offender is *Alleys of Eden*, a poignant tale of the last days of Saigon. Cliff, an American deserter, returns to "the world" with Lanh, his Vietnamese girlfriend. Once in the United States, their relationship finally falls apart, much as, one would suspect, Alden Pyle's and Phuong's would have if Graham Greene had allowed Pyle to survive in *The Quiet American* (1955). The point is that their differences are not so much explored as they are just erected as a dramatic wall to separate them.

The Tears of Autumn and *The Defector*, although written specifically about the Vietnam War, fall into well-recognized and more general types. *Tears of Autumn*, about a plot of the Ngo family to both restore themselves to power and to revenge themselves on the Kennedys for the assassination of Ngo Dinh Diem, reads more like a Robert Ludlum thriller than an intimate experience in Vietnamese culture. The book is full of Vietnamese kinship structures and reveals some of the Vietnamese fixation on horoscopes, but this Orientalia only furnishes the clues that uncover the plotters, allowing the hero Christopher Hubbard to escape, while the reader is left with another pieful of Oriental mystery in his face.

The Defector is another John Le Carré type of spy thriller (like *The Spy Who Came in from the Cold*), set, however, in Hanoi rather than behind the iron curtain. Like Le Carré's work, the spy here is involved in some double business, and, at the end, he shares the fate of his more famous "cousin" Alec Leamas in dramatically failing to come in from the cold. The book does have a good analysis of Vietnamese communism and hints at the family ties that persist despite the ideology. Again, this is all part of the mystery.

A more genuine, if delightfully improbable, novel is Loyd Little's *The Parthian Shot* (1973). This also is a Mekong Delta novel that takes place during the Adviser War. A Special Forces team is placed upriver in the remote heart of the land of the Hoa Hao (a politico-religious sect). The American command loses track of the team, and it becomes a part of the Hoa Hao's armed forces. Hoa Hao culture is richly described, and the whole novel comfortably revolves around the concept of yin and yang, putting our American "black-and-white" thinking, comparatively, in stark and ridiculous relief.

In a class by itself is Donald McQuinn's *Targets*. Although somewhat flawed as a novel—it has a distracting subplot that is never resolved —McQuinn weaves a spellbinding tale of an elite joint Vietnamese-American intelligence unit intent on smashing the shadowy Viet Cong infrastructure in Saigon. Specifically, it is the story of an American colonel who recruits the remarkable Major Charles Taylor to track down the wily Binh, a high-level Viet Cong cadre. Thanks to an uncanny and almost innate empathy for Vietnamese culture and psychology, Taylor dramatically gets his man. In the process, the complexities of the war are highlighted with unusual clarity. For openers, the choking chaos of Saigon receives one of its best descriptions ever. Also, the labyrinth of the Viet Cong's organization and modus operandi is peeled apart with the same eye for detail as Francis West, Jr.'s nonfictional *The Village* (1972). In addition, the cultural barriers to the romantic interludes between Vietnamese women and American men are explored in ways that are only hinted at in other works like Graham Greene's *The Quiet American*. And, finally, the Vietnamese-American "counterpart" relationship is plumbed more thoroughly than even in Halberstam's *One Very Hot Day*.

What emerges in *Targets* is the most sympathetic portrayal yet in the literature of the travails of a South Vietnamese nation slowly betraying itself. What also emerges is that one of the barriers to an American appreciation of this Vietnamese agony, and indeed of an understanding of the war itself, was the in-and-out twelve-month tour by which American servicemen experienced Vietnam's generation-long struggle as a mere, though often searing, spasm in their own lives.

As has been mentioned repeatedly, thus far most of the literature on the Vietnam War draws heavily on the personal experiences of the authors.

But these experiences are only slices of the whole, and the whole is never merely equal to the sum of its parts—it transcends them. This, of course, is a dilemma that confronts all literature. In the case of the Vietnam War, though, it is more than the atomistic battlefield that has to be transcended. The war was also a clash of cultures, ideologies, and societies in different stages of historical development. How these larger themes have been played out in the United States has received some attention in the literature, but their play in Vietnam, by and large, has not.

It was a completely different show in Saigon, and it can be instructive (even for the imagination) to look at the war from the other side of the theater. To begin with, John Clark Pratt's seven-act play of the American involvement in Vietnam from 1941 to 1984 would just be one small act in the drama of all Vietnamese history. Just how ephemeral the American involvement in Vietnam was to the Vietnamese was brought home to me in Saigon on March 28, 1973, the last day of the sixty-day U.S. troop withdrawal period called for in the Paris Peace Agreement. In going to one last Chinese movie, I found the film stripped of all its English subtitles, while the Vietnamese, Chinese, and French remained.

Actually, to the Vietnamese the Americans were just part of the act of modernization brought to their society by the age of imperialism. With this age came Frenchmen, communists, Americans, sectarian revivalists, and men and women with competing traditional and modern views of nationalism. In the French sociologist Paul Mus's apt phrase, it was a culture pushed "off-balance" into the twentieth century. Thus, while in the United States the epithet of our involvement as imperialistic was a matter of sharp domestic debate, in Vietnam it was not. Such involvement was just part of the act.

It was an act that produced a maelstrom of international and internal struggles within Vietnam. There were the grand themes: the international struggle between American containment and Maoist people's war, of modernists propounding democratic and constitutional principles versus what Alexander Woodside called "Mandarin Proletarians" who ultimately sought to modernize their Confucian ethics with Marxism-Leninism. There were the riled-up Buddhists who raged at the West, disdained the communists, burned themselves in the streets, and, ultimately, didn't know what they wanted.

There also were more poignant personal struggles that encapsulated many of these larger themes. There was the Catholic, Confucian Ngo Dinh Diem whose proud family sought to steer South Vietnam away from Marxist-Leninism with a nationalism that was an incongruous blend of French personalism and old-fashioned Vietnamese cronyism. The effort ran afoul of the venerable Thich Tri Quang and his enflamed Buddhist bonzes. Dismissed by some as a dupe of the communists, Tri Quang was much more of a cross between Cardinal Richelieu and Mahatma Gandhi. Seeing himself as the Vietnamese Gandhi, his machinations made more people recall the Machiavellian French cardinal. Though Diem is dead and Tri Quang is now under house arrest, the story of their struggle is still waiting to be told. If a future writer wants to avoid the fate of Asa Baber and requires an American hero, he can include some facsimile of Lucien Conein, the CIA agent who got himself tangled up in the middle of this encounter.

On the other side, there was the very intense and barely kept-within-bounds debate over strategy as the communists struggled for a plan to deal with the influx of American forces from 1964 to 1968. The outlines of this debate, as portrayed by Patrick J. McGarvey in his *Visions of Victory* (1969), makes fascinating reading. After reeling from some large and bloody battles (to wit, the Battle of Ia Drang Valley in November 1965), General Vo Nguyen Giap deemed it prudent to avoid such engagements and build his forces up for a shock attack somewhere, sometime later. This posture was intensely frustrating for Nguyen Chi Thanh, Giap's commander in the field, who wanted to keep going after the Americans before they became too well established in their huge logistical enclaves. Farther south in the Mekong Delta, communist commanders argued for a more protracted guerrilla war strategy until everything could be sorted out. Though not forgotten, the debate was swept aside by Nguyen Chi Thanh's untimely death in the fall of 1967 (some say to an attack of pneumonia or of cancer while others say to a B-52 raid around Khe Sanh). Giap's triumph, ironically, was the debacle of the Tet Offensive, saved as being perceived as such only by the wholly unexpected reverberations from the offensive in domestic American politics. Certainly there is a gripping novel to be had here.

In offering this small sample of stories for literary exploitation, I am trying only to make the point that, if it ever was, the Vietnamese experience is no longer "closed to us." There is an ample literature now on such figures as Ngo Dinh Diem, Thich Tri Quang, and Vo Nguyen Giap to permit portrayals of their and other Vietnamese personalities in far more substantial terms than cardboard. If, in trying to write about Vietnamese, they still look at us with "numb stares," then we have illiterate imaginations.

The way to overcome this cultural illiteracy is to begin to appreciate the context of the Vietnam War *in Asia*. I have just suggested that this Asian context consists of the bewildering social, political, and economic forces unleashed on Asian lands by Western imperialism, a context that now manifests itself as a crisis of modernization. Just as some veterans of the Vietnam War like John Del Vecchio have sought meaning and enlightenment in literature, so also the Vietnamese have turned to their literature and cultural tradition for meaning and stability in the face of the twentieth century's buffeting storms. The first place that every Vietnamese turns to is the all-time classic of Vietnamese literature, *Kim Van Kieu*, written by Nguyen Du in the beginning of the last century on the dawn of the French arrival.

In the *Kieu*, Nguyen Du takes a threadbare Chinese story and turns it into a Vietnamese masterpiece. He portrays a young heroine's attempts to maintain her virtue in a world turned topsy-turvy. When the world is finally righted, although her virtue is restored, a happy ending cannot be fully effected. Too much has happened to be completely forgotten or forgiven. As the story goes, Kieu is a young Vietnamese beauty betrothed to the noble Kim. A sudden reversal of fortune forces Kieu into a life of prostitution to save her father. Political upheavals follow on Kieu's misfortune, and she finds herself under the protection of the romantic bandit chieftain, Lord Tu. Tu offers her an opportunity for revenge on her several tormentors. Kieu is mostly generous, but not completely. Tu has a big heart, but he is brutal. Ultimately he is killed. Kieu is finally reunited with both her father, proving herself to be a filial daughter throughout her travails, and with Kim, her still noble but somewhat languid suitor. Kieu is left with some burdens from her past, including memories that the mechanics of her profession were not always "a fate worse than death." She agrees to stay with Kim, but not to live with him conjugally. For this side of life she allows Kim to marry her sister. *Kim Van Kieu*, then, is hardly a fairy tale. It is a cultural war story. Also, if the participants of this conference have a penchant for ambiguities and quandaries, so, too, do the Vietnamese. For the Vietnamese, the torments of the modern age are all in the *Kieu*.

If the basis for an understanding of the Vietnam War can be found in the larger context of Western imperialism and the anguish of modernization flowing from it, then "large canvas" novels of the war, I believe, are possible. The British have certainly developed a rich literature around their imperial experience. The works of Rudyard Kipling, Joseph Conrad's *Heart of*

Darkness and *Lord Jim*, and, especially E. M. Forster's *Passage to India*, as examples, have done much to capture the spirit of empire.

One always has to be careful with contexts, however. The brush might be too broad. In viewing the Americans as imperialists, as essentially all Vietnamese did (whether positively or negatively), certain dangers of perception existed. With this perspective, the Vietnamese communists feared that even if the South Vietnamese government fell, the Americans would never abandon their bases in Vietnam: Marble Mountain in Danang, Cam Ranh Bay, Long Binh. Equally for the South Vietnamese government, it developed a sense of security around a belief that no matter how corrupt its administration, the United States could not afford to lose these positions. What stunned *all* Vietnamese was that the United States could sit on its hands and watch it all go down the tubes in fifty-five lightning days. If we were imperialistic in Vietnam, ours was an imperialism of policy, not of possessions. When the policy went bankrupt, the possessions lost their meaning. This brings to the surface yet another irony of the Vietnam War: the Vietnamese never understood *us* either.

All of this is to say that adding the Vietnamese dimension to the Vietnam War allows Tim O'Brien's circling birds to cover the full ambit of the war and provide the grounds for its dramatic truth. Maybe truth with a capital T is too high a summit, but like Apollo 8, which never landed, at least we can see the far side of the moon.

5   Truth—Whither Goest Thou?

The Role of Literature in Understanding the War

—America lost her virginity in Vietnam.
—(And she caught the clap, too)
—That's nothing—so did I.
—I did too, but now I watch who I go out with.
—So should America.
GI *latrine graffiti*, Saigon (*cited in Pratt*, Vietnam Voices)

The final session of the conference, on "The Role of Literature in Understanding the War," was, in many ways, the payoff for the tensions that came with the lightning bolts. It was the most thoughtful moment of the conference. Passions were spent and the participants turned reflective.

In creating this mood, Bill Broyles served as the moderator of a panel of three men known for their abilities to synthesize and pull things together. In gauging the place of this literature in bringing about an understanding of the Vietnam War, their skills were fully taxed, and demonstrated. They are all eclectic figures: both men of experience and men of letters. Bill Broyles himself is a marine combat veteran and a former editor for *Texas Monthly* and for *Newsweek*. Phil Beidler is also a Vietnam combat veteran. He served as a reconnaissance platoon leader in an armored cavalry troop. More recently, he has written an acclaimed book on *American Literature and the Experience of Vietnam* (1982). James Chace has had a varied career, starting as a young artist writing a novel in Paris, a city in 1954 under the shadow of the fall of Dienbienphu. Later he turned to foreign affairs and eventually came to be the managing editor of *Foreign Affairs*. Currently he works for the *New York Times* where, among other things, he reviews a lot of books. John Clark Pratt, the final panelist, told the conference that he is a blend of nine personalities—a collage really—ranging from an air force fighter pilot in Laos to a professor of English at Colorado State University. He is also the author of *The Laotian Fragments* (1974) and compiler of *Vietnam Voices* (1984).

In this concluding session Bill Broyles, in "exploring the geography of his heart," found a great deal of confusion, in himself and in the conference more generally, between the personal and the political. This has led him to a great ambiguity over the war, an ambiguity only heightened by a recent trip back to Vietnam where he toured the now eerily silent "fields of fire" in which he once fought. Phil Beidler spoke of literature's truth and of its potency in changing society. James Chace, on the other hand, initially resisted this mixing of art with politics but came to realize, as he tried to write a novel in France during the siege of Dienbienphu in Indochina, that the two were inseparable. Regarding the American war in Vietnam, he felt we could talk only of consequences, not of lessons. On a hopeful note, Mr. Chace was optimistic that literature could achieve, if not resolution, at least some reconciliation. More pessimistically, John Clark Pratt thought that, with the current confusion and complexity over fact versus fiction, there can be no whole to the Vietnam War and thus the best literary form for an understanding of the war is the collage. Navigating between these shoals of optimism and pessimism, my essay will suggest ways in which this literature might improve its and society's understanding of America's longest and most difficult war.

The Asia Society's conference on the Vietnam Experience in American Literature caught Bill Broyles at a time of ferment over his own experience in Vietnam. Since making a four-week return trip to Vietnam in the fall of 1984 and in leaving his job at *Newsweek* shortly thereafter, "I've been wrestling with what this war has meant, and I've been exploring the geography of my own heart." Going back to Vietnam and seeing its geography again, and its people strangely at peace, opened his eyes to a lot of things he should have seen before, but also left him with very confused and ambiguous feelings.

For the first time in public he told the story of his near desertion before being sent to Vietnam. At the conference Tim O'Brien and Stephen Wright told similar stories. Bill Broyles put his uniform back on and got on his flight because he knew his contemplated desertion would be an act of cowardice and not an expression of antiwar convictions. Tim O'Brien caught his flight to Vietnam because, in his mind, he was too cowardly to desert. Both men served in Vietnam with distinction.

To Broyles, at the center of this ambivalence to the war is "the connection between the personal and the political, and how all of us still have the two confused. I think that this has been particularly true in the cases of Jim Webb and Ron Kovic and Al Santoli and a lot in me . . . it is very hard to go back and forth between what happened to us and what it all means for everyone else." This ambivalence stems from the dilemma that though art and politics may be inseparable, their sources of knowledge are different.

As he said further:

> **Broyles:** So much great art is rooted in human suffering and intense human experience. That is, I think, one of the basic foundations for the knowledge we get as human beings: it's suffering. But I'm not sure what a guide it is to our politics. Whether it is what Ron Kovic is suffering personally . . . or whether it is the suffering of the Vietnamese that Al Santoli writes about, both these sufferings are real. But I don't think either really tells us where we should go as a people necessarily. Somehow we have to be able to engage other parts of our being and transcend that suffering and figure out what we do next.

Or, as Tolstoy once put it, a quote that John Clark Pratt used as the preface to his *The Laotian Fragments*: "There are two aspects to the life of every man: the personal life . . . and the elemental life of the swarm, in which a man must inevitably follow the laws laid down for him." The problem in moving from the personal to the political is that the significance of the personal disappears and gets lost in the swarm. As Broyles found: "The war is over now. . . . We are, and this may be very hard for us to accept, a small part of their [Vietnamese] history now. They are a very ancient people, and we are a blip on their screen already. Maybe we'll come to the day when Vietnam is a small part of our history."

In returning to Vietnam a second time, Bill Broyles stumbled into an encounter that, I think, brought his soul home. In a conversation with the Viet Cong general against whom his marines fought, the communist leader thanked Mr. Broyles for his antiwar activities after he returned home. Unexpectedly, Broyles got mad and kindled this exchange:

Broyles: I didn't do this for you! I didn't think that you would be good for Vietnam. And I still don't. But I thought we were worse; plus Vietnam was terrible for us.

General Tuan: Yes, it is right that you should love your country too.

Speaking of "coming home," in giving his talk Phil Beidler suddenly realized that it had been fifteen years to the day since he returned home from combat in Vietnam. Since then, he said, "I have had the blessed fortune not only to have come home, but to spend the rest of my life to date inquiring into the means whereby people use language and other sign systems to make sense of themselves and of their relation to the world." In this, Beidler has come to the conclusion that literature has great powers in offering this general guidance that Bill Broyles seeks in transcending his personal experience. Beidler's thesis is simple: literary language creates its own truth in a dimension where distinctions between fact and fiction do not obtain. This dimension of literary language is what makes us human because it is the dimension in which we make connections between words and things; it is where we find meaning to our lives and the world around us. We put things in relation to each other. But stepping outside ourselves to see these patterns is difficult—like trying to spell God with the wrong blocks—and risky. To Beidler, though, the only literature that lasts is the literature of risk. It is literature that points up unusual connections. As an example, he cited this passage in Gus Hasford's *Short Timers* (1980) of a soliloquy by an infantryman during a break in the Tet Offensive's battle for the imperial capital of Hue:

> I love a little commie bastard man. I really do. Grunts understand grunts. These are great days we are living bros. We are jolly green giants walking the earth with guns. The people we wasted here today are the finest individuals we will ever know. When we rotate back to the world, we're going to miss having somebody around who's worth shooting. There ought to be a government for grunts. Grunts could fix the world up. I never met a grunt I didn't like.

In this unusual connection we see the bond of mutual respect among those baptized in the fire of combat, a respect that even crosses over to the other side. It was this mutual respect that Hasford grasped in his novel that so amazed Bill Broyles when he actually encountered it in his visit to his former enemies in Vietnam. It is in connections like these that literature reveals its transforming power. Beidler concluded with what was the strong-est statement in the conference about literature's political power.

Beidler: We truly can be transformed, and even possibly be redeemed by electing to write of times, of what happened—but also of what might have happened, what could have happened, what should have happened, and maybe also what can be kept from happening or what can be made to happen. . . . Words are all we have. In the hands of brave and true artists such as those we have heard here, they may yet preserve us against the darkness.

Thus again in this conference we see Plato's truth: "Art is politics."

In his speech James Chace admitted that he was a little slow in grasping this truth. In his early years he felt that art would always be adulterated by politics if the two ever came together. So after graduating from college, he went off to the pristine literary atmosphere of Paris to write the great novel. Unfortunately, the Paris that Mr. Chace ran into was the Paris of 1954, and this was not a good time to be in Paris to write politically celibate literature. The death of France's *mission civilisatrice* was oozing from the mud of the doomed French bastion at Dienbienphu. Students took to the streets, berating the French presence and demanding of the French commander, "Navarre to the gallows" because he, too, had talked of "light at the end of the tunnel."

Mr. Chace got caught up in these riots and eventually got his unjust reward from the rather ungenerous French police. After he picked himself up from the pavement, he realized, "Wait a minute. This isn't my war. We don't do this sort of thing in America." He also realized that "the idea of literature engagé was a reality. Literature was important. It did change things." He decided, then, to return home and find out about American politics.

In concentrating on America's foreign relations, Mr. Chace's attention returned again to Indochina. Looking now in 1985 over the wreckage of America's war in Indochina, he has been struck by two ironies. To Chace, now that the drama is all played out, it is ironic that the game was over before it began. It ended in 1954 at the Geneva Conference that closed the curtain on the French presence in Indochina. Had everyone at that conference, including the Americans, abided by its provisions, the tragic game need never have been played. The other irony lies in all the talk over the loss of American credibility as the result of its Indochina debacle. To the contrary, Chace feels that at least to our European allies our credibility was in question *because* of our involvement in Vietnam on behalf of a losing cause in an area so peripheral to our interests. Hence, our credibility only improved after our withdrawal.

Though Chace had less to say about the stock of American credibility in countries less distant from Vietnam than Europe, he did say that the massive extent of our commitment and the frustrations over its lack of success has led to such division over the war in American society that there are no agreed-upon lessons on the nature of the U.S. intervention. Lessons or no lessons, he argued that, nevertheless, there have been some unmistakable consequences. The most obvious, as demonstrated by this lack of lessons, is the breakdown of the cold war consensus that undergirded postwar American foreign policy. It was broken by the Tet Offensive of 1968 in Vietnam and is still reflected in our foreign policy today. Such a cold war consensus, Chace is quite confident, will not come back soon.

Also, as a result of Vietnam, for the first time in its history the United States can no longer think of itself as an exception, or at least as a moral exception, to the normal rules governing the behavior of nations. In our actions in the war—the bombing of the North, the Christmas bombing of 1972, the invasion of Cambodia, and in the secret bombing there—the means exceeded the limited ends we sought, and we thus came to behave like other nations in the past. In Vietnam, the United States "became an ordinary country." Chace's hope is that we will, as a result, also become a more mature one.

Finally, a consequence for being a divided nation over the Vietnam War has been a legacy of bad feelings toward its veterans. This, Chace strongly feels, should not be the case. It is in effecting a reconciliation between society and its veterans that literature can play its most constructive political role. In effect, Chace said literature could do this by making sure the veteran wasn't stuck with the blame for the first two consequences.

> **Chace:** I think there is a feeling of reconciliation among people: not to blame those who fought an unpopular, wrongly conceived war. In this sense literature can best aid us toward that reconciliation. It will tell us that such a war cannot be made to seem other than it was. It was not a glorious enterprise, but a tragic experience.

Thus, in undertaking this political mission and in highlighting the war's moral ambiguities, to Chace, the literature on the Vietnam War "is the most important we have to deal with right now."

If there were those at the beginning of the conference who were jolted and offended by the intrusion of James Webb's politics into the conference, perhaps Mr. Chace's speech served as a justification for *their* views. Obviously, though, many had not waited for Chace's speech before jumping into the political fray on their own. Meanwhile, it can be said that Chace, from his poststudent days in Paris, has come a long way in overcoming his aversion to politics.

To return to literature itself for a moment, juxtaposing James Webb's keynote address with the remarks of James Chace (or with any of the other pairs of polar-opposite sparring partners at the conference), we are confronted once again with John Clark Pratt's dilemma of "one man's fact being another man's fiction." Indeed, in bringing it up again, Pratt immediately got into a squabble with Myra MacPherson over whose facts were the biggest fictions. But MacPherson's objections really served only to dramatize his point, that a solution to this dilemma is beyond us. No one can read enough, even of what's already been written. Thus, in some instances, people are calling for a type of work that already exists. In others, they are demanding writing that cannot be done.

Pratt sensed a tremendous stretching of effort and intellect at the conference. In recalling some of these efforts, he also provided a cogent summary of the conference itself:

> **Pratt:** By way of reviewing the conference, . . . I have just been writing comments as they go along:
>
> —Mr. Chace's comment yesterday that one must define the problem first, define what it is before we can look for solutions.
>
> —The comment which I have mentioned about Ho Chi Minh as a poet but also as a very dedicated, determined, and ruthless leader.
>
> —C. D. B. Bryan's comment about the problem with facts, about getting the facts together.
>
> —Mr. Lomperis's comment earlier about the larger context and the need for perspective.
>
> —Ron Kovic's, how are we going to learn this business?
>
> —Mr. Broyles's comment, the best of the literature will last.
>
> —Del Vecchio's comment earlier about coordinates and how to show the multiple perspectives.
>
> —And then the question about does one have to have been there to write well about it?

How do we take this multiplicity, this incredible complexity, and have it make sense at all?

Pratt went on to say, "There is no whole to the Vietnam experience." If so, James Chace is right: we have no lessons, only consequences. Even though we all may have our favorite, and often contending, consequences, John insists that there is an answer to his question. There is a literary form to put the war in some kind of pattern and make sense of it. It is the collage.

The collage is built on the premise that "we cannot perceive the totality of contemporary existence. All we can perceive is its multiplicity, and it scares the hell out of us." Applied to the fiction of the Vietnam War, the thread that Pratt sees running through all the works is the word "fragments." With this concept of fragmented perception, which Pratt sees everywhere in our society "in the way we go at everything from art to public affairs," the contemporary artist or novelist showers you "with a whole bunch of fragments and lets you figure out what happens." In this form the author actively engages the reader in the interpretation of his story by not telling all of it, by not filling in all the details. What makes these collages difficult for the author is that, in surrendering part of his story to his reader, the author has no idea what this strange character, the reader, is going to do with his story. The facts the reader may draw on to make his conclusions and finish the story may be totally different from those of the author. But this is precisely what the collage ultimately leads to: a blending of fact and fiction to the point where the two are indistinguishable and achieve a fusion. To John, this is the whole purpose of the collage: "I would hold that to understand the Vietnam War one must somehow see a fusion in fact and fiction and . . . knowing both, look beneath or behind or around them for the truth of the experience itself." The alternative, he implies, is to believe only what other people tell you is the truth.

Mr. Pratt received some vindication of his having contributed to an understanding of the war in Laos, as well as showing the potency of the collage, in his novel, *The Laotian Fragments*. Initially he had trouble getting the air force to take his work seriously when he approached its office of information about problems the novel might have with classified material if it were published. The immediate response was, "We don't review fiction. If it's fiction, go ahead and publish it. That's no problem." When they took a closer look, they slapped a top secret cover sheet on it. It took ten months for the air force to clear the "facts" for publication as fiction. And the facts or the fictions or both—the fusion, in fact—certainly had their effects. A week after the book was cleared, Pratt received a very curt and anonymous phone call:

> Hello, Colonel Pratt?
>
> Yes.
>
> I cannot tell you who this is, Colonel Pratt. However, I want to let you know that your novel has changed the foreign policy of the United States toward Laos. Thank you very much.

This call only confirmed in John Clark Pratt's mind that "there is no difference between art and politics." But, Pratt said, "this is something Ho Chi Minh knew all along."

For Lady Borton and Myra MacPherson, all this talk of the collage, indeed often of the literature as a whole, thus far had been on too intellectual a level.

> **Lady Borton:** I have felt a lot of confusion in the last couple of days. . . . I'm not one of the guys, and yet I am a returnee. I am also not an intellectual. I make my living driving a school bus. I go round and round in circles.
>
> **Audience person:** So do we.
>
> **Lady Borton:** I've done it for fifteen years: round and round. And I get real confused here because this is so intellectual, and I'm not part of that world. I think for me responding to the Vietnam situation, and from having been around on all the different sides of it and particularly more on the Vietnamese perspective on it, is that what I come out with are not ideas, but feelings. I am so struck by the absence of the word feelings in this conference. . . . At least for me, the feeling was one of weeping, and I'm not a crier. It was weeping for individual people, and not for a mass. I guess I just want to encourage us as we look at this experience to go down to the feeling level of it and . . . allow ourselves to weep for individual Vietnamese people, regardless of which side they were on and where the blame for the war should lie.

Myra MacPherson echoed this.

> **MacPherson:** You know, I agree with Lady. What bothers me is the incredible bisecting on a level that has nothing to do with the really fine fiction that people have written here, where they really do get into

the feelings of people. And in my oral history, I have people who talk remarkably like the people that I read in the fiction. And these are real human beings.

On this, at least, Phil Beidler was able to offer reconciliation.

Beidler: I think we haven't talked about it because it was a given. It was a subtext. This is all incredibly passionate literature. That's what makes it important. It makes the rest of modern experimental fiction look like head games. These are people who write books that get into your guts.

To John Clark Pratt's fusion of the fact and the fiction, no one objected to adding a third element, and making of this fusion a trinity of fact, fiction, and feeling. Though the conference weighed fairly heavily on the sides of fact and fiction, feelings were certainly not absent. As someone in the discussion said, "There has been a lot of weeping." "Yes," agreed Myra, "I think there has been a lot of that here." In fact, as both Arthur Egendorf and Bill Broyles pointed out, this conference, and the individuals thrown together to make it up, was a beautiful expression of John Clark Pratt's collage. It was beautiful because, as Al Santoli said, "Everybody is coming from a sincere place."

With respect to the art form of the collage, I would be papering over too much if I closed here. People at the conference expressed their reservations. Lady Borton was confused. Myra MacPherson said she never really understood what John Clark Pratt was talking about. Bill Broyles was impressed, but skeptical. The level at which Mr. Pratt finally connected on his art form was when he stooped to illustrate what the collage could do when seen through the broken pencils and scratchy Bics of the anonymous authors of the war's latrine graffiti, "something," he said, "which the Vietnam War really gave our heritage." Pratt spoke movingly of his unsuccessful endeavors with his military superiors to preserve these literary monuments in situ. Nevertheless, despite the repeated whitewashing of the latrine, Pratt succeeded in saving a few samples of what he called "progressive graffiti" for the chapter headnotes to his book, *Vietnam Voices*.

It is through stories like this that we can reach the heartwarming conclusion that nostalgia is not yet dead in America. For the untold number of Vietnam veterans who relieved their tropical discomforts in the entertaining company of the scatological Socratic dialogues of the "Shithouse philosophers," these etched witticisms will always be remembered as the fleeting frescoes of the American Empire. And, as I hope the headnote to this chapter attests, they had their truths to tell.

Essay   The *Iliad* and the *Kieu*: Building Understanding

Paul Fussell, in his *The Great War in Modern Memory* (1975), talks of "recognition scenes" in which in certain poignant moments, like in a traumatic war or social upheaval, we see ourselves, as we most essentially are, in what we do. In building a greater understanding of the Vietnam War, and of ourselves through our literature, there are some things about ourselves we need to see.

Perhaps the most obvious feature of this literature is the centrality of politics. If a hallmark of American society is its apolitical discourse and aversion to ideology, the language of the Vietnam literature runs strongly against the grain. Of course, the war itself was a highly politicized one and the literature, which is still largely coming from its participants, can hardly be expected to run away from this fact. Yet politics in art needs a subtle expression, and much of the literature thus far has been too self-conscious about its politics. Bill Ehrhart is certainly not unique among these writers in his candid confession that he considers his writing a failure if it does not serve his "educational" purposes. More bluntly, Ron Kovic wants people to think as he does. So does Al Santoli. Since, to put it mildly, these two don't think alike, there is a problem.

There is another problem with politics in literature: however clear his political message may be to the author, the political effect of any literary work is often uncertain. Arthur Miller, for example, intended his play, *The Crucible* (1953), to be a scathing indictment of the McCarthyism raging across the country at the time. Only a few got the point. But literature, nevertheless, does have a superb play about the Salem witch trials.

If politics is inseparable from literature, particularly in the case of the Vietnam War, then it is important to recognize that literature is not immune from the manipulations of politics and, sadly, may even serve many moral masters. During the conference John Balaban gave us the memorable line, *"Rhetoric makes people killable; literature makes people believable, and lets them live."* It's a memorable line but it just "ain't necessarily so." The contradiction to this lies in the very poem of Ho Chi Minh, "On Reading 'Anthology of a Thousand Poets,'" with which Balaban concluded his talk:

> The ancients loved those poems with natural feel:
> Clouds, wind; moon, snow. Flowers, rivers, crags.
> A poem should now contain strong tempered steel;
> A poet, now, should learn to lead a charge.

I am not convinced that Ho Chi Minh wrote this just because he loved a poem, as Balaban argued. Revolution is what I think he had unmistakably in mind. Freed from the Kuomintang prison in which he wrote this poem, the charge he ultimately led through the phalanxes of Frenchmen, Americans, and his own countrymen cost over two million lives.

When a man reaches a point in his political convictions that it becomes moral to kill, as all politics of the swarm inevitably do, then it is not too large a step to a little poem like this one, the first three verses of the national anthem of Democratic Kampuchea, "Glorious April 17th":

> Bright red Blood which covers towns and plains
> Of Kampuchea, our Motherland,
> Sublime Blood of workers and peasants,
> Sublime Blood of revolutionary men and women fighters!

> The Blood Changing into unrelenting hatred
> And resolute struggle,
> On April 17th, under the Flag of the Revolution,
> Frees from slavery!

> Long live, long live Glorious April 17th!
> Glorious Victory with greater signification
> Than the times of Angkor!

If John Balaban were to insist that this is a flagrant piece of rhetoric and not poetry, I would be the first to agree with him. But 150 years ago there were doubtless some Englishmen who thought that Francis Scott Key's little poem about "bombs bursting in air" was also an obscene piece of rhetoric. In politics, one man's rhetoric is another man's poem.

This is why Plato many years ago wanted to banish poetry from his *Republic*. Poems, kernels of truth that they may have, are nevertheless emotionally volatile and can kindle hate as readily as love. Such passions distracted a philosopher from his rational pursuit of wisdom and should, therefore, be banned. Even though subsequent history ignored Plato's warning and sacrificed a little wisdom to keep its poetry, it is still important to recognize that good literature and good politics will not always be coterminous.

However, if it is a given, in this literature anyway, that art is politics, or at least that politics cannot be fully separated from art, then the writers of this literature can profit by becoming better informed about the political side of the war. There is, quite simply, an enormous body of works in the prosaic world of facts that can enrich any author's understanding of the Vietnam War, and of Asia. Since this point was made often in the conference by others, most notably by Asa Baber, John Del Vecchio, John Clark Pratt, Al Santoli, and John Balaban, I need not belabor it. But it might be worthwhile to highlight some of the better works.

There are, first of all, superb interpretive books on the Vietnam War, and they are sufficiently diverse now to satisfy all political palates. Most cover specific periods or aspects of the war, but there are some more general ones that do provide *a* sense of the whole. For the history of Vietnam we are fortunate to have the writings of Joseph Buttinger, William Duiker, David Marr, Truong Buu Lam, and Alexander Woodside. For those who want to read the "Ho Chi Minh line," the major work is by Le Thanh Khoi, who writes in French. On the appeal of Marxism-Leninism to the Asian peasantry, the best works are by the China scholars Lucian Pye and Richard Solomon. Frances FitzGerald's *Fire in the Lake* (1972) applies some of their insights to Vietnam. A more academic treatment of the Vietnamese peasantry is Samuel Popkin's pathbreaking, *The Rational Peasant* (1979). On the organization of the Viet Cong itself, there are the illuminating works of Douglas Pike (1966) and William Andrews (1973). In my view no one has yet done a better job in laying out the conceptual struggle between the Viet Cong and the Americans than Jeffrey Race in his *War Comes to Long An* (1972).

On the supposition that some writers may be more interested in building their works around some of the people involved in the war rather than around such grand themes as communism, nationalism, and the Mandate of Heaven, there is a rich literature in this area as well. Memoirs or biographies are now available on such principal figures as Kennedy, Johnson, Nixon, and Kissinger. Works are also out on Ho Chi Minh, Vo Nguyen Giap, Le Duan, William Westmoreland, and Maxwell Taylor. Neil Sheehan is still at work on a biography of John Paul Vann, America's star military adviser. Moving away from these more visible personalities, all of the military services have oral history libraries with tapes of the debriefings of the senior American and South Vietnamese military officers. For the local Viet Cong there are the incomparable 1,500 Rand interviews with communist prisoners and *Chieu Hois* (ralliers to the government side).

There are documents literally everywhere. Besides the *Pentagon Papers*, every government agency involved in Vietnam is busy compiling its history from this sea of documents. For its eighteen-volume study the U.S. Army's Center for Military History has an entire warehouse of largely uncatalogued documents in Suitland, Maryland. With all this raw information, it cannot be said that the Vietnam experience is closed to us, but it certainly is scattered.

The real problem in understanding the Vietnam War is not a dearth of information or facts. There are facts aplenty, even about the Vietnamese. The problem is bringing all these scattered bits together and arranging them into patterns that have meaning and can tell a coherent story. The impasse lies in how to do this, an impasse that John Clark Pratt describes so well in his *Laotian Fragments*:

> How little we really know about other human beings from the incon-clusive fragments that they let us see. Yet how much we *think* we know. Perhaps the real tragedy of today is that we mistake bits and pieces for fact. Too much information—thus massive ignorance. But we have to make decisions anyway. So what do we do? Flip coins. Roll dice. Guess. Ignorance breeding impulse: What grand ingredients for truth. (p. 188)

Pratt uses this impasse to suggest the art form of the collage as a better way for understanding the war than flipping coins or rolling dice. The problem with the collage, at least with respect to the Vietnam War, however, is that it assumes too much on the part of the reader. In involving the reader in figuring out the collage, and fusing the fictional with the factual for an underlying truth, Pratt is counting on the reader's own ability to grasp the context, find the allusions, and see the symbols. Untutored by the author, I am not sure that ability is there. This problem is rendered doubly difficult by the fact that the author (having no overall answer) may be resorting to the collage to mask his own shaky grasp of his subject. It seems to me, for the collage to do a significantly better job than flipping coins or rolling dice, it needs to have a larger frame put around it to serve as a guide for at least an improved understanding of the subject. In fairness, Pratt does do this in his own work.

In the case of the Vietnam War such a frame should ideally combine the traditions and literature of both East and West. To consider these other human beings that we know so little about for a moment, at some point it needs to be recognized that the interactions between Americans and Asians in Indochina were largely a male-female exchange. It is only a slight oversimplification to say that the Americans (91 percent of whom—to cite a favorite conference statistic—were male) shot the men and hustled the women. These contacts seemed simple on the surface but could get very complicated underneath. In the *Laotian Fragments* is a poem of one of these contacts, "Words and *Thoughts*," in which an American pilot fails to move in on his fallen comrade's Thai girlfriend:

> Hey, you, *you slant-eyed, luscious brown-skinned broad,*
> Why you no smile tonight? What you no hab?
> Where your zoomie tealoch-man who keep you,
> Pay you, love you? He butterfly around again?
>
> Maybe he go home States and send for you.
> Big joke. It neber hoppen. He buddy me.
> He hot jet jockey, sure, but he hab wife,
> Three baby-san. He short-time. He speak lie.
>
> No worry, babes, no sweat. I tell you true.
> *You have long legs, great calves, soft, rounded thighs.*
> *You need no Hongkong bra.* You number One.
> You nice girl. You not nit-noy. You super-Thai.
>
> I same-same. No hab mama-san like him.
> You be my tealoch, I extend a year.
> I make love good—always use balloon.
> I long time love you mach mach—chai?
>
> *Don't cry, please. I'm so sorry.* I no try
> To hurt you. I just make damn silly joke.
> *I'm a lonely pilot, very far from home.*
> *Who plays the game.* I dumb GI.

Your tealoch good man. Marry you someday.
Please, what's the matter? What you say?
He shot down? He work Tchepone today?
I didn't know. Flew last night. Slept all day.

You loved that part of him he let you love, I know.
But so did we.
Please stop your crying and forgive us all,
As well as me. (p. 190)

Surely there is a grand novel in the making here that could elaborate and elevate this tragic barroom scene around a frame that meshes the *Iliad* and the *Kieu*. Here our modern Patroclus can hardly wait to fill the pants of the fallen Achilles in caring for the stricken hero's surviving and forlorn mistress, Kieu, as the siege of Troy continues. Perhaps this is a bit overdrawn, but the point is, there need to be more allusions in our literature. This is basically Paul Fussell's criticism of the American literature that came out of World War I. As excellent as this literature was, it suffers in comparison to the British literature because English writers anchored their works with references and allusions to other great pieces of literature.

Where indeed would such literary giants as Shakespeare and Milton be without their rich allusions and metaphors drawn from the Bible and Greek mythology? These very allusions tease out the ironies, make the metaphors vivid, and create the strands of meaning for making sense out of the jumble at our feet in the present. The allusions can draw on a culture's traditions for a context at the same time as they preserve these traditions through their continued use. For example, a future poem about an Army "lifer" in Nam, who is furious over a newspaper account of a group of antiwar demonstrators' early release from detention and the general effect these demonstrations are having on the combat morale of this unit, could do no better than have his "lifer" call these demonstrators "jackals" in an allusion to D. H. Lawrence's novel, *Kangaroo* (1923) about World War I: "At home stayed all the jackals. . . . And they bit us all. . . . We should never have let the jackals loose, and patted them on the head. They were feeding on our death all the while" (p. 241).

In the literature on the Vietnam War, works that do make these references and allusions stand out for having done so. What makes Bernard and Marvin Kalb's *The Last Ambassador* so full of dramatic tension is its rich detail, a detail derived from Frank Snepp's nonfictional account of the frenetic last days in the Embassy, *Decent Interval* (1977), and the North Vietnamese commander General Van Tien Dung's account of his victorious campaign, *Our Great Spring Victory* (1977).

The novel that builds the most on previous works is John Clark Pratt's own *Laotian Fragments*, a novel that is the epitome of his collage. What holds the fragments of his collage together is the figure of York Harding, the political science professor who receives the dossier of fragments that tell the jagged tale of Major William Blake, missing in action over Laos. York Harding, one recalls, is the "author" of *The Advance of Red China*, *The Challenge to Democracy*, and *The Role of the West*: the books that in Graham Greene's *The Quiet American* proclaimed the ideology that sent Alden Pyle off to Saigon as a "soldier of democracy."

To return to John Clark Pratt's quote about facts, we cannot surrender to complexity with a roll of dice. This is a denial of our very humanity, and I'm sure that Pratt agrees. After all, Major Bill Blake of *The Fragments* is shot down while trying to win a part of the war *his* way. Since leaving the Garden of Eden, we have lived our lives by our choices, based on the best information we have. We are able to make these choices by using our values and our traditions to put this information in some order of importance to us. God and divine revelation told us this once. For some, God still guides. As for the others to whom God is lost, they must use their values to weigh what is more right, more beautiful, and more true, and then rely on their courage to see their decisions through in an agnostic world where truth is only partial. Indeed, this faculty for decision—for making truths out of facts for purposeful action—we have made the pride (and occasionally the fall) of our species.

With respect to Vietnam, we have enough facts. What we lack is the courage to make our values explicit and subject to scrutiny by others. When some do step forward—like James Webb, Ron Kovic, Bill Ehrhart, and Al Santoli—we walk away, embarrassed, and not yet ready to face what is the real Gordian knot to the understanding of the Vietnam War: not complications over unfathomable facts but a deep-seated clash over values. Rather than face this, we cling to our more socially amenable ambiguities, as the artistic and social resolution to the Vietnam War continues to wait.

In the world of events, in 1985 the remains of some thirteen Americans missing in action were released by the communist government in Laos. In the world of fiction, perhaps York Harding, now a venerable professor emeritus, could make a last trip to Southeast Asia to pick up the remains of the by now thoroughly fragmented Major William Blake. There the professor can reminisce about the colorful pilot, and about Alden Pyle, and about America's generation that marched off to Southeast Asia. It is time for some truths to come from this early professor of containment, whose writings did so much to send forth these "soldiers of democracy." He must speak to us, now that it's over.

My only warning is that if his speaking is too overtly political, no one will listen. He should speak not as in his younger years when he wrote *The Role of the West*, as if he were the Oracle of Delphi, but as a more sober, somewhat self-doubting Socrates, stumbling over his facts, but surer of the values that still have stood the test of the awful reality of America's longest and most difficult war.

Conclusion

America's Future in Asia (and at Home)

"It don't mean nothing, man. It don't mean nothing." – Bill Broyles, on the veteran's standard response to his Vietnam experience

A central concern of The Asia Society in this conference was to render an assessment of the literature of the Vietnam War in bringing about a greater understanding of the war and of America's future role in Asia. While the conference did not assess this future directly, many of the issues raised certainly bore on it. John Balaban talked of the United States as a global power that inevitably would be drawn into conflicts elsewhere, such as in Central America, and hence of America's need to come to a basic understanding of its war in Vietnam. Indeed James Webb's keynote address was a call for both an artistic and a societal resolution to the war. All of those at the conference seemed to accept the inevitability of a future American war, but not a war as ambiguous as the one in Vietnam. With such a plea, it can only be appropriate to conclude with an essay that attempts to provide at least a broader context for such an understanding. This essay, then, will briefly discuss the Vietnam War and its literature in terms of the larger pattern of U.S.-Asian relations. Specifically, it will examine our understanding, and lack of understanding, of Vietnam as provided by both a foreign policy of containment and a literary tradition growing out of existentialism. Mention also will be made of the Vietnam War's destruction of mutual trust in American society, the more salutary record of U.S. relations with the Philippines (as a possibly hopeful antidote to a preoccupation with

Vietnam), and of the importance to our country in seeing ourselves—and the Vietnamese—clearly in this war, in part through a new body of literature that seeks, from an already solid foundation of individual experience, a larger vision of truth.

The Asia Society's conference on the literature of the Vietnam War began with the keynote speaker recalling Plato's adage, "Art is Politics." That observation touched off howls of protest. As the conference wore on, it became clear that it was not Plato's adage, but James Webb's politics themselves that provoked the protest. One of the most vociferous protestors, William Ehrhart, for example, readily confessed to his own political muse. Indeed, the lightning bolts of this conference (James Webb, Ron Kovic, and Al Santoli), whose outbursts did so much to define the boundaries of the discussion, were political rather than literary. If Plato painted with too broad a brush in his assertion, in the literature on the Vietnam War anyway, the passions animating it *are* distinctly political.

James Chace discovered the high content of politics in literature as he struggled to write a novel in Paris with the reverberations of the fall of Dienbienphu all around him. *Literature engagé* they called it in France. At about the same time (or shortly before), U.S. policymakers had concluded that America's long-standing tradition of isolationism could no longer be sustained. World War II had made the United States finally conscious of the great power it possessed and of the implicit responsibilities to the amorphous international system that came with that power. With the titanic world struggle against fascism still fresh in everyone's mind, a similar and more ominous struggle loomed against a nuclear Soviet Union and its ideology of communism. A determined American public united behind the doctrine of containment, fashioned by these policymakers (George F. Kennan, Paul Nitze, and Dean Acheson among others) for an interventionist America. The United States, then, became a *puissance engagé* that received its highest expression in John F. Kennedy's 1961 inaugural address—"We will bear any burden, pay any price to ensure the success of liberty"—that so fatefully charged the idealism of a generation of young Americans, among them Ron Kovic.

Fate kept America to its word, and in the jungles of Vietnam its sons began to pay the price. Containment, as a policy, held up well along the iron curtain in Europe. But its application to other parts of the world, particularly to Asia, was vague and not too well thought out. George Kennan, who saw the world in geopolitical terms and hence was acutely aware of the limits to American power, sought to confine the direct application of containment to strongpoints of national interest, which included (after the fall of China) only Japan in Asia. Occasionally, for historical reasons, mention was made of the Philippines. The immediate post-World War II vision was based on what Akira Iriye (1974) called the Yalta System, which was built on notions of an independent China guaranteed by a balance of power (particularly of outside powers) in East Asia. In this system, Southeast Asia was left to the responsibility of the colonial powers: the British, French, and Dutch.

By 1950 this hazy system had been washed away by a rippling tide of events. In August 1949 the Russians exploded an atomic bomb, which conveyed visions of a global reach to Soviet power. In October 1949 China fell to the communists. Southeast Asia in this setting beckoned as a power vacuum. The British had given independence to India, Pakistan, Ceylon, and Burma. The Dutch had withdrawn from Indonesia. And the French were locked in a revolutionary war of independence in Indochina with the communist Viet Minh. In June 1950 the North Koreans invaded the south. This invasion was almost universally perceived in the United States as being launched at the instigation of the Soviet Union. With this perception, Munich was quickly recalled, and the doctrine of containment reached out to embrace Asia. Dominoes seemed on the verge of falling everywhere.

Kennan's successor on the National Security Council was Paul Nitze, a man with a less geopolitical view of power than Kennan. Nitze sought to explicitly incorporate nuclear weapons into American national security strategy. In his view, and certainly in the view of others, such a strategy would be unencumbered by the limits of Kennan's geopolitics, and the reach of American power would be truly global in scope. Little, judicious nuclear threats would make every point a defensible strongpoint, even remote places in Asia.

Metaphorically, or globally, this all looked beautiful from the air, but even at the beginning in Asia, containment, once on the ground, became snarled in national and geopolitical realities. The Korean War (1950–53) itself severely strained American conventional military capabilities to the point where afterward some army officers formed a "never again" club. In Indochina, after taking a good hard look, the United States drew back from launching a nuclear strike (and even a conventional air attack) to save the French at Dienbienphu in 1954. Nevertheless, despite these growing signs of limits, by 1955 Secretary of State John Foster Dulles completed the forging of a chain of treaties literally around the world, committing the United States to the defense of fifty-four nations. In the 1960s the earlier success of the communist Viet Minh in Indochina in 1954 and of Fidel Castro in Cuba in 1960 raised the specter of successful communist insurgencies elsewhere: in Colombia, Venezuela, the Congo, Burma, Laos, and Vietnam—even though in Greece, Malaya, and the Philippines such insurgencies had failed. After sending several fact-finding missions, and buoyed by some successful standoffs with the Soviets (most notably the U.S. triumph in the Cuban missiles crisis of 1962), the United States extended the dikes of containment to Vietnam and Laos. Armed with the self-confidence of the Kennedy administration's "vigor" and the wisdom of an imposing literature on counterinsurgency theory, it was to be another marine fifty-mile hike, with Harvard dons as drill sergeants.

Once on the ground in Vietnam, the dikes and hikes of containment turned into a morass. Rather than a gung-ho charge up a San Juan Hill, the intervention became more like the Chinese proverb's "journey of a thousand miles," with the difference that the "single steps" seemed to be leading nowhere. The government of South Vietnam was hardly a bastion of freedom, and it was embarrassingly apparent that in some quarters of Vietnamese society the Viet Cong were genuinely popular. Ron Kovic felt raped, and even Fred Downs, who was basically supportive of the war, looked in vain for reassurance that he was doing the right thing. As so much of the literature on the Vietnam War has given such moving testimony to, it was, in the words of the dying Kurtz (from Joseph Conrad's *Heart of Darkness*), a "horror."

As the war progressed, it was made more horrible by the compounding blindness of the rising and increasingly strident antiwar movement. Many observers have commented on an innate American tendency to think in black and white, good and evil terms. Thus for the Presbyterian Secretary of State, John Foster Dulles, nonalignment with a superpower in the heyday of the Cold War was impossible because, "He who is not for me is against me," and the struggle with the Soviet Union became not just one of power but a moral one between "the children of light and the children of darkness." In reverse, the same became true for the antiwar movement. If, for Daniel Ellsberg, President Lyndon Johnson was perpetrating a "crime" in Southeast Asia, it did not take long for the demonstrators to start waving Viet Cong flags, though Ellsberg himself shied away from such a gesture. If

South Vietnamese leaders Ngo Dinh Diem, Nguyen Cao Ky, and Nguyen Van Thieu were fascist dictators, it did not take long either for Ho Chi Minh to become the patron saint of all the good hearts who gathered at the Washington, D.C., mall.

In this, these youthful demonstrators of the 1960s were only being smitten by a more recent strain of an old virus of the left, the agrarian reformer myth. It started with Mao Tse-tung and the line of Western reporters who trekked to the Yenan Caves in the 1930s—Agnes Smedley, Barbara Tuchman, Edgar Snow—and brought back stories gushing of Mao's nationalist and reformist aspirations for his backward people. While these aspirations were certainly true, what these reporters did not dwell on at any length was that Mao's aspirations were also communist. The same set of aspirations were true as well for Ho Chi Minh in Vietnam and Pol Pot in Cambodia (now Kampuchea). Although such remiss may be merely embarrassing to yesterday's antiwar activists, these "realized" communist aspirations are now part of the daily sufferings of the still backward peoples of Indochina.

In recounting a roughly similar record of blindness in the American interaction in East Asia over two centuries, James C. Thomson, Jr., Peter Stanley, and John Perry conclude in their recent book that the recurring theme in this interaction, whether from the right or the left, is one of "virtually invincible ignorance" (1981, p. 309). This is in large part because, in the central contention of their book, American imperialism was not due to a bloodlust for territory or conquest, or, for that matter, for plunder or economic advantage; rather, for the Americans "their inexhaustible fuel was sentiment" (p. 311). Hence their title, *Sentimental Imperialists*. Unfortunately, sentiment requires only good intentions, not information. Indeed, too much information may be too confusing to these intentions.

It is sad to have to say that, with respect to Asia and the Vietnam War, literature, in the main, has only compounded this political ignorance. During the conference several participants commented on the narcissism and relativism of the Vietnam War's literature. Fred Downs, in particular, called for the authors to move beyond their personal experiences and to address larger themes. In contemplating this, most participants felt that the telling of the absolute truth on the war was beyond them. Certainly all felt that the Vietnamese dimension would be difficult, and in fact was something most of them had shied away from. As Bill Broyles said, "The Vietnamese experience is closed to us." At best, these authors could offer a partial, or relative, truth. Interestingly, for all these problems, few writers were ready to give up on "truth" completely and go off with Tim O'Brien and rest content with "fictive truth's" standard of the good story.

The central contribution of literature to America's "invincible ignorance," however, stems from the very nature of existentialism as much as it does from an ignorance of the Vietnamese themselves. By the time the literature on the Vietnam War was being written, the weltanschauung of existentialism had come to dominate virtually all of modern literature. Whatever the variations from author to author, those with an existentialist worldview hold that the only experience whose authenticity one can be sure of is one's own. Everything else, life itself, is absurd, or devoid of meaning. Not that other lives do not exist, but to pretend to know them is absurd. This leads to a pessimism, or at least to a disinclination to do or learn much about the rest of the world. The result is a turning inward to self for meaning. Everything else falls away—institutions, countries, cultures, even values —and what is left is everyone atomistically "doing his own thing."

There is a perhaps unintended but nevertheless pernicious political side effect to all this artistic introspection. Existentialism developed in the West, and there is the prosaic fact, then, that the people espousing this philosophy were from politically powerful and materially wealthy societies. As they scrutinized themselves, they ignored others. Perhaps it was not with the same studied and racist ignorance of the classic imperial sahib, but they demeaned other people, including those of other societies, by viewing them, in philosophic and indeed in existential terms, as "nonpersons." This "ignorance" received its most insensitive expression in Albert Camus's *The Stranger* (1954). Set in Algeria, the novel focuses on the personal reactions and thoughts of a French colonial (resident) whose difficulties in "relating to his environment" lead ultimately to indifference. So supreme does this indifference become that one very hot day the "hero" becomes so feverish and thirsty that he shoots an Algerian native out of mere exasperation.

In the West *The Stranger* was taken as a powerful philosophical statement. Perhaps inhabitants of the Third World can be forgiven if they saw less of the philosophy and a good deal more of the no doubt unintended but nevertheless implicit racism in the work. In fact, for whatever reason, this tendency to "not see" people of other races, that is, to not accept them as fully human, is what has fueled the rage of both American blacks and Third World colonial subjects. The need for cathartic violence as the only solution to this oppressive indifference received chilling utterance in Eldridge Cleaver's *Soul on Ice* (1968), for American blacks, and in Frantz Fanon's *The Wretched of the Earth* (1963), for the subjects of Western colonies. Besides the blinders of containment, Vietnam became no stranger to reincarnations of the indifferent ignorance of Camus.

Before moving on to the prospects for the future, in this little litany of ignorance, I must confess that I have overdone it a bit. James Webb is right, we are our own worst critics. Americans *have* had a soft spot and an awareness of Asia for over two centuries, as the authors of *Sentimental Imperialists* have noted. For all their sentimentality, Pearl Buck's *The Good Earth* (1931) and Christine Weston's *Indigo* (1943) brought an awareness to American homes of China's and India's teeming millions and crushing poverty. Alice Hobart's *Oils for the Lamps of China* (1933) kept alive the myth of China's unlimited markets. On a popular level for Asia as a whole, the voluminous writings and compilations of Lin Yutang (*The Wisdom of China and India*, 1944) made him the Oriental equivalent of Will and Ariel Durant.

Other works provided more penetrating portrayals of Asian peoples. On Japan, in the prewar period the writings of Lafcadio Hearn stand out as does, especially, Ruth Benedict's *The Chrysanthemum and the Sword* (1946),* which gave World War II GI's such an excellent pulse of their Pacific enemies. After the war Edwin O. Reischauer became the informal dean of a strong group of American scholars on Japan. Western scholarship on India has always been impressive from the groundbreaking works of Max Müller in the nineteenth century to the more modern writings of A. L. Basham and Percival Spear. Western, and particularly American, writing on China has been so extensive that I almost hesitate to mention anyone because of the long list of those left out whom I will offend. For their insights into Chinese culture, however, few can fault me for singling out the works of John K. Fairbank and Joseph Levenson, who did the bulk of their writing in the 1950s and 1960s. There was even some familiarity with Indochina. In the 1940s and 1950s Virginia Thompson, Bernard Fall, and Paul Mus were laying the groundwork for the body of writing of today. And as I and many of the conference participants have acknowledged, much of this literature, both fiction and nonfiction, is very good, even in rare instances, on the Vietnamese.

*Professor Benedict wrote many of the insights that went into this book for the U.S. Army before the war.

It is also important not to lose sight of the fact that, for all the parade of fools spotlighted by David Halberstam in his *The Best and the Brightest* (1972) and by Barbara Tuchman in her *The March of Folly* (1984), the United States has been served by some very brilliant diplomats and astute analysts of Asia. Although George Kennan was the first to admit that he lacked expertise in this vast continent, he felt there were those he could count on for this expertise, including John V. A. MacMurray who argued in 1935 against a total war with Japan because it would upset the balance of power in Asia (1984, pp. 51–52). Easily in a similar league during this period was the American ambassador to Japan, Joseph Grew, and the four Johns in China (John Carter Vincent, John Paton Davies, John Stewart Service and John Emerson), as well as the salty general, Joseph W. Stillwell.

Indeed, as has been well documented by Russell Fifield (1963) and Evelyn Colbert (1977), these and the immediate postwar analysts of Southeast Asia fully recognized the potency of nationalism in the region and the importance of being on the right side of it. Virtually all of them also strongly recommended that the United States takes pains to disassociate itself from colonialism in the region. These analysts, however, were less clear on what the United States should do if the local communists also were on the right side of nationalism, as they uniquely were in Vietnam. Unfortunately, more global (that is, European) imperatives of containment forced the United States to side with the French in the latter stages of their struggle with the Vietnamese communists (1950–54), which later put the United States right in the way of this nationalist juggernaut during its involvement in the Vietnam War. David Halberstam to the contrary notwithstanding, Leslie Gelb, in his prize-winning *The Irony of Vietnam: The System Worked* (1979), argues that American foreign policymakers in the Vietnam War era actually realized all of this, especially that national priorities ultimately lay elsewhere, and both devised and implemented a strategy that at least successfully prevented the United States from suffering an outright defeat. (Just parenthetically, whatever salve this book may have offered to these beleaguered policymakers, it has not offered much solace to the nation as a whole.)

Having said all this in deference to the criticism of our excessive self-criticism by James Webb, the general pattern of American relations with Asia still remains one that has been more dominated by ignorance—or at least unrealistic judgments and distracting suppositions—than by insight. Whatever flashes of insight there have been, have been fitful, or, more importantly, fitfully received. "Europe first," or some version of it, has always won out in American foreign policy circles. This pattern, further-more, has only been abetted by a literary tradition that has turned intro-spective and is, in effect, also "Europe first."

The only consistent exception to this pattern, and, perhaps, then, a hopeful beacon for the future, is the American record in its only former Asian colony, the Philippines. Whatever the controversy surrounding the United States' acquisition of this colony in the Spanish-American War (1898), William Howard Taft's shrewd policies of "attraction" were instru-mental in defeating an insurrection against American rule and securing the cooperation of the Filipinos for the rest of this rule until independence in 1946. Taft's mix of political carrots and military sticks is well portrayed in John Gates's *Schoolbooks and Krags: The U.S. Army in the Philippines, 1898–1902* (1973). (Curiously, no one appeared to recall this relatively more happy experience when the United States was searching for guiding parallels and analogies in Vietnam.) After a humiliating ejection from the islands at the start of World War II, General Douglas MacArthur heroically returned to the Philippines as a liberator in 1945. After independence, a U.S. military assistance team provided sage advice and helped coordinate a successful counterinsurgency campaign of the Philippines government against the communist Huk insurgents. Most recently, despite the rather indecent length of America's tacit support of the Marcos regime, by all accounts the indirect but instrumental role of the U.S. government at several levels in helping to bring about a peaceful transition to the new government of President Corazon Aquino was adroitly done.

Perhaps there is something to be said, then, for the advantages to a long, sustained experience with a particular country and people, something Americans never had in Vietnam, but did have in the Philippines—and may have in Central America. Unfortunately, sustained experience is not the only key to wisdom—as the long, tragic experience of the French in Indochina has shown.

To return more centrally to the American agony in Vietnam, in addition to being a clash of arms, the Vietnam War was also a clash of facts, and of values. Much of the literature on the war has only made this worse by being, itself, so individualistic and atomistic. The tragedy is that David Winn may not have been right enough about the American soul: more than split by Vietnam, it may be splintered. If this is so, then the wound of the American defeat in Vietnam may be more serious than we have thought.

Several conference participants talked about having split personalities over the war. James Webb spoke of the tensions in being both an official of facts and a writer of ambiguities. Bill Broyles lamented over the confusion between the personal and the political in trying to resolve the war. Broyles and others also related their moral anguish as they got the jitters sorting out their values the night before they flew off to the war. The worst case, though, was John Clark Pratt who claimed to have to percolate the Vietnam War through nine personalities. Perhaps not quite as bad as John Clark Pratt, on a larger tableau Vietnam has given the United States a case of the jitters, or at least of confusion, over its future role in the world. The bipartisan consensus that undergirded the foreign policy of containment has broken down. In their surveys of American opinion leaders in 1976 and 1980, Ole Holsti and James Rosenau have found, in *American Leadership in World Affairs* (1984), that these leaders are now split among three groupings of opinion: traditional isolationists (who see the primary threat to American security arising from unresolved domestic issues), unrepentant interventionists (who regard the Soviet military challenge as the primary threat), and post-Cold War internationalists (who want an America still active in world affairs but one that focuses on North-South issues and channels its activism through multilateral forums). Upon these three disparate pillars, no coherent post-Vietnam War foreign policy has yet been built. Analysis of a third survey of these opinion leaders in 1984 has shown a persistence of this same three-way split.

While the United States dithers, the Vietnamese have had to face some cruel splits of their own. In marrying their nationalist aspirations (for independence against the French and for socialist reunification against the Americans) with the distaff intellectual side of the large cultural onslaught of the West, the Vietnamese communists have found their borrowed Marxism-Leninism to have served their purposes well. During the conflict it served to galvanize the rising expectations of the masses and to gather them around the party. But with both wars over, and the romance of insurgency having been replaced by the more prosaic yoke of incumbency, the Marxism-Leninism of the Vietnamese rulers is not meeting the now risen expectations themselves. Marxism-Leninism sure made good war, but making good peace is not proving to be one of its specialties. From their crushing military triumph eleven years ago that so riveted the attention of the world, Ho Chi Minh's successors today rule a country that is largely out of war, out of work, and out of view.

In terms of Asia as a whole, the dominant legacy of the Vietnam War is that it represents the end of the traumatic transition to the postcolonial world. The Vietnam War effectively put an end to imperialism by Western powers in Asia. The United States, though, remains a Pacific power. Through its enormous volume of trade with East Asia and through the simple demographic fact that two-thirds of the world's people live in Asia, the United States will always have to be concerned with that continent. But, because of the Vietnam War, it can never control or "come to the rescue" again—at least by itself.

In Asia, then, the United States can no longer be a master; but it can be a model. In running afoul of people's war in Vietnam, the United States still remains a beacon of people's rule. Perhaps here lies a continued vocation for America that can be salvaged from the wreckage of Vietnam and redeemed for the future. Ironically, what adds a note of hope to this new, or really very old, vocation for America is the consolation that the Russians, too, for all their ships in Cam Ranh Bay, are likely to find their Asian role to be limited to that of a model as well.

America's war in Vietnam represented, if not the longest, at least its most intense contact with Asia. It also prompted the most searching reexamination of the morality of U.S. civic life since the Civil War. The war "over there" permeated all levels of American society (even among those who did not participate) and scarred an entire generation. To this point, not much of the Asian dimension to the war has become part of our experience "over here." Yet if our future is in part in Asia and an understanding of this region is therefore important, one pathway to this understanding is through a literature of the Vietnam War. Whether we, as individuals, liked the war or not, protested it or supported it, for this scarred generation that is now coming to power in America, the Vietnam War is the undeniable gateway to Asia—and to ourselves.

In the realm of politics the Vietnam War should have made it clear that the United States can no longer act on global policies that are blind to, or ignorant of, local realities. American literature, similarly, if it is politics, or at least informs the suppositions with which we engage in politics, can no longer serve this political ignorance by wallowing in the narcissism of individual experience and of relative truth. Politically, such a literature only feeds an arrogance of power. Literature, if it is to elevate our politics—to see things that only it can see—has to embrace truths beyond individual experience. Without such truths beyond ourselves there would be no collective identities or common human values—or "sympathies" as the Chinese sage Mencius called them—to appeal to. Indeed, there would be no purpose to language if it could not do what it is supposed to do: provide a network of categories that link the experiences of our own with those of others to give both utterance and meaning to our humanity and to the larger truths and insights that can come from the sharing that language and literature allow.

If for the nineteenth-century philosopher Søren Kierkegaard, one of the founders of Christian existentialism, the authenticity of his humanity could come only from a deep introspection into the hopeless gap between God and himself and to nevertheless trust to His goodness, to the contemporary Walker Percy this authenticity and wholeness can come also from relating to other people through language and literature. A writer, then, is one who uses language to shake and draw the souls of others to him for a sharing of communicable ideas and experiences—in the form of a history, essay, novel, poem, or play—to enlarge our understanding of a particular problem or set of dilemmas that confront us all. Such a process requires a confirmation of at least a good part of what is being said in the words, experiences, and insights of others. We can only accept these confirmations by restoring our faith in the one value most shattered by the Vietnam War, *trust*. Much of the quarreling over facts and statistics in this conference really had more to do with bitter memories over a sense of being lied to or propagandized during the war, whether by the U.S. government, by slanted journalism, or by a literature fostering "the Ho Chi Minh line."

In his keynote speech James Webb reported that Vietnam veterans are more likely to marry, own homes, and have a family than a normal sample of the population. As the group most shattered by the Vietnam War, perhaps this is because they have come to realize, with Walker Percy, that the only way back to their humanity after the war is to commit themselves to other people again, to *trust*. There is a message in all this for today's writers. If they want to reach for truths greater than themselves, they will have to trust and build on the experiences and insights of others: of their combat buddies, certainly, but also of people different from themselves —like the Vietnamese—and even disagreeable to them—like James Webb, Ron Kovic, and Al Santoli.

Myra MacPherson concluded, after all her interviews with Vietnam veterans, that the wounds to their souls will not heal until a catharsis on the war is reached that faces all these differences. True. It is also true that Vietnam is an historical experience that still carries enormous significance for the interpretation of present events. Vietnam is conjured up at every crisis where the threat of American intervention looms. But it is invoked in such contradictory ways that its only effect is paralysis. For some it is a curse that must be exorcised, while for others it is a sacred warning. The Vietnam War is an historical experience that is clearly in need of some final judgments so that some resolution can be achieved. Such a resolution is not a mere academic exercise. It will determine when, if, and under what set of conditions my son and others will go to war. The conference did yield to Plato's other unrelenting dictum, "Only the dead have seen the end to war," but in so doing it also appeared to want to be sure that there would be "reassurance" that the need would be compelling enough and convincing enough for the living not to remember the dead with a crushing burden of guilt.

I have called James Webb, Ron Kovic, and Al Santoli lightning bolts to this conference because their outbursts (or speech and two outbursts) revealed a good bit of what must be confronted in achieving resolution and drawing lessons from the Vietnam War. They said some diametrically opposite things that were quite unambiguous. As I have said before, not all facts are arithmetically equal. It is time to strip off our cloaks of courteous ambiguity and make some judgments about which facts are right and which are wrong, which insights are better and which are "off the wall," what still really is ambiguous, and what literature grabs our souls and rings true.

As I touched on earlier, Paul Fussell wrote about countries and individuals finally recognizing their unburied selves in the traumatic act of war. What do we recognize of ourselves in Vietnam when, as Bill Broyles said, the dominant quote of the returning Vietnam veteran has been: "It don't mean nothing, man. It don't mean nothing."? But that has always been a lie. When it "don't mean nothing," it means, in Broyles's translation, "everything." It's just that no one yet has been able to express it fully. Certainly some have rendered powerful expressions of parts of it. But all of it still has to come out so we can face ourselves with honesty; and Asia—and our future—with wisdom.

Bibliographic Commentary

"From the Fiction, Some Truths"

by John Clark Pratt

In her *Newsweek* essay of 25 February 1985, Meg Greenfield stated that "too many people . . . are blinded and tyrannized by their memory" of the Vietnam War "and refuse to take its illumination. They are unwilling to reinspect what happened and what is happening because that means reinspecting and perhaps reappraising their own past role and belief" (p. 96). Characterizing many Vietnam authors, veterans, protestors, and other members of what John Wheeler believes is a generation that has been "touched with fire," Greenfield is of course correct.

However, there is another and broader dimension as well. What of the new generations? What of those who while growing up caught only glimpses of a TV war? What of *their* children, those who will have no memories by which to be "blinded and terrorized"? How will *they* also learn about and come to grips with the sheer fact of the United States at war in Vietnam? Just how does one either form or "reinspect" his or her view of America's longest and most divisive war?

One can, of course, read "history," but by mid-1986 there are only smatterings of references in standard textbooks, four interesting but hardly complete single volume works (Michael MacLear's *The Ten Thousand Day War*, Stanley Karnow's *Vietnam: A History*, Timothy Lomperis's *The War Everyone Lost—And Won: America's Intervention in Vietnam's Twin Struggles*, and James Pinckney Harrison's *The Endless War*), and the first few (of fifteen) volumes in the Boston Publishing Company's series *The Vietnam Experience*. In addition to numerous picture books, there are also the three editions of *The Pentagon Papers* ("Official," Senator Gravel, and *New York Times*)—eighteen volumes in all, with each edition containing material not present in the other two and all stopping with the events of 1967—and Gareth Porter's massive, politicized collection of primary materials, *Vietnam: A History in Documents*. If one wishes, he or she can read the multitudinous monograph memoirs being published by the various armed services' historical branches, or, if one dares, consult the millions of microfilmed and hardcopy documents available in each service's libraries. Or, one can dive in and read any of the hundreds of individual historical and political works published during the last forty years, but choosing this option is much like entering Dante's Inferno without a guide.

One also can, and this possibility seems quite ironic to me, watch television, either the thirteen-episode PBS or the shorter CBC series, each of which has moments of brilliance that are sadly offset by periods of intense political myopia. Finally, I must mention that one could at least start with my *Vietnam Voices*, which presents a collage of many "factual" and "fictional" perspectives, arranged chronologically, to *introduce* (but only introduce) a reader to a search for understanding.

There are, of course, the growing number of excellent oral and personal narratives: from the earliest *Vietnam Diary* (1963) by Richard Tregaskis; Jim Lucas's *Dateline: Vietnam* (1966); Elaine Shepard's *The Doom Pussy* (1967) (which the author claims is really a novel); James Jones's *Viet Journal* (1974); Donald Kirk's *Tell It to The Dead* (1975); C. D. B. Bryan's *Friendly Fire* (1976); Gloria Emerson's *Winners and Losers* (1976); Philip Caputo's *A Rumor of War* (1977); Tim O'Brien's *If I Die in a Combat Zone* (1973); Michael Herr's *Dispatches* (1978); Al Santoli's *Everything We Had* (1981); A. D. Horne's edition, *The Wounded Generation* (1981); Wallace Terry's *Bloods* (1982); and Robert Mason's remarkable *Chickenhawk* (1983). Most recent is Truong Nhu Tang's fascinating *A Vietcong Memoir* (1985). Each of these is immensely valuable and in the aggregate would provide a reader with an overview of how the Vietnam War was experienced by each of the perceptive authors and contributors.

Obviously, some mixture of all of the above would provide a broad exposure to the reality of the Vietnam War—but to understand and apprehend the truth (which after all is the only real fact) of the war, I suggest, as Michael Stephens so well put it at the Westside Y conference of 1984, that one can best learn about the Vietnam War through the works of art: the poetry, drama, and fiction written about and by Americans in Southeast

Asia. The more than 200 novels (with more in the presses), the hundreds of short stories and poems, and the few excellent dramatic works show not only the history and the politics but more significantly the human drama of those who were involved. Most important, however, is the fact that art demands interaction by the reader. Reportage can well present someone *else's* view, but the experience of reading fiction, poetry, or drama draws the reader in and makes one as much a part of the experience, as Hemingway once noted, "as if he were there." As John Updike notes in the August 1985 *Esquire*, "Unlike journalism, history, or sociology, fiction does not give us facts snug in their accredited truths, to be accepted and absorbed like pills, for our undoubted good; we *make* fiction true, as we read it" (p. 62).

There are many individual short stories and collections, but four works stand out: the propagandistic but fascinating *The Fire Blazes* (Hanoi, 1965); *Free Fire Zone* (1973), edited by Wayle Carlin and others; *Writing Under Fire* (1978), edited by Jerome Klinkowitz and John Somers; and *Enemy Country* (1984), by Emilio de Grazia. For drama, David Rabe is unquestionably *the* playwright of the war, with his *The Basic Training of Pavlo Hummel* and *Sticks and Bones* (1973) prefiguring some of the themes of his current Broadway show *Hurlyburly*. Also significant for its satire is Barbara Garson's *MacBird* (1967) and Amil Gray's *How I Got That Story* (1981) for its depiction of the elusiveness of any kind of truth. Finally, Tom Bird and the New York theater group VETCO have presented plays of merit.

In poetry, two writers predominate: John Balaban and W. D. Ehrhart, with Walter McDonald and Bruce Weigl having also published Vietnam poems of the first rank. Most of the poets who wrote about the war did so immediately to protest the war, and as such, their poems are of historical interest but are not always successful as art. Ehrhart's large body of work, however, including *A Generation of Peace* (1975) and *To Those Who Have Gone Home Tired* (1984), best show in his stark, clipped verse the feelings of a combat soldier at war and at home. His poem, "A Relative Thing," expresses the feelings of *all* Vietnam veterans, regardless of their views about the war. Addressed to Americans as a whole, the poem concludes:

> We are your sons, America,
> and you cannot change that.
> When you awake,
> we will still be here.

Balaban's poems are richer, more complex and universal, and unlike most of the other artistic works written about the war, concern themselves with the Vietnamese as well. In *Vietnam Poems* (1970), *After Our War* (1974), *Blue Mountain* (1982), and the translations, *Ca Dao Vietnam* (1980), Balaban's poems range from the realistic to the mystical, from the profane to the spiritual. Whether they be about a Saigon bar girl typing a letter to her American lover,

> i think about you all time
>> you alays in myha heart
> make love na
>>> make. love. not. . war . . . .
> fuck. . . . . you
>> Monique

or the obscene acronyms of his realistic prose poem "Monthly Report—Agriculture," Balaban's work shows an impressive vision of all humanity engulfed by war.

So too do poems by Walter McDonald, like Balaban and Ehrhart also a writer of fiction, in *Caliban in Blue* (1976) and *Burning the Fence* (1981). Also of growing importance is Bruce Weigl, whose most recent volume, *The Monkey Wars* (1985), contains some moving poetry set in Vietnam. Poets such as D. C. Berry (*Saigon Cemetery*, 1972) and Dick Shea (*Vietnam Simply*, 1967) should also be noted, as should the anthologies *Winning Hearts and Minds* (1972) and *A Poetry Reading Against the War* (1966).

It is from the fiction, though, that the real truth as well as the real progression of the war best can be seen—but there are problems. Not everyone can visit the Colorado State University's Vietnam War Literature collection and sit in the only room in the world where all the published works of fiction, poetry, and drama are available in one place.* How to start reading the fiction seems just as challenging as the task of approaching the historical and political works, so what I would like to present here is a way to respond to Greenfield's plea for "reinspection" and also to address my concern (I am now a college professor) that today's younger Americans know absolutely nothing about the Vietnam War, even when the most earnest of them compare it with events in Central America. An example: I recently saw *The Killing Fields*, and after the theater lights

---

*This collection is, by the way, an ongoing search, and it includes manuscripts. All queries and submissions are welcome.

came up, a young woman in front of me asked her friend, "Was that real?" The reply: "I wasn't sure, but they put the dates on at the end, so I guess it was."

Because the vast amount of Vietnam War literature is just beginning to be comprehended, only a few substantial works of literary criticism have emerged, most of them Ph.D. dissertations. Much of this scholarly analysis, however, is understandably limited by the authors' selective processes. Often intentionally, many critics have omitted or ignored works that do not seem to fit their personal views of the war. Perhaps part of the problem is the literary critic's penchant to search for patterns (and I too will be guilty in this essay); but altogether too prevalent, as with Michiko Kakutani's derivative, truncated 1984 *New York Times Book Review* essay or Samuel Freedman's pop-art gloss in the *New York Times Magazine* (11 March 1985), the real reason for presenting a superficial view seems to be a critic's understandable (but no longer forgivable) ignorance and sloth. Such is the severe problem with James Wilson's *Vietnam in Prose and Film* (1982), in which the author notes that "forty to fifty Vietnam novels have been published" (he was less than one-third right) and that the war caused "hundreds of thousands of American deaths" (pp. 4–5).

There is also the problem of deadlines, of course. Since the American publishing industry began to gear up for the impending anniversaries of cease-fire and collapse, critics and reviewers who have been confronted with the need to say something quickly have made "definitive" judgments based on hasty scanning. One of the better Vietnam novelists, Jack Fuller, for instance, in his 1982 *Chicago Tribune* essay, "War in Words," mentions only *one* Vietnam poet (ignoring W. D. Ehrhart and John Balaban); then, while noting the "elements of fable" present in *Going After Cacciato, The Barking Deer,* and *The Bamboo Bed,* does not acknowledge such equally "fabulous" works as Asa Baber's *Land of a Million Elephants,* Loyd Little's *Parthian Shot,* Ward Just's *Stringer,* MacAvoy Layne's *How Audie Murphy Died in Vietnam,* and Pierre Boule's *Ears of the Jungle.* Fuller's main point, moreover, that "the best novelists, at least while the war was being fought or painfully vivid in memory, realized that they could not confront it head on" (p. 65) seems more to define his own problem with the literature than it does to show the attitudes of the novelists themselves.

Of the serious critical studies that have been made, five stand out: Peter Leonard Stromberg's pioneering dissertation; Margaret E. Stewart's "Death and Growth: Vietnam-War Novels, Cultural Attitudes, and Literary

Traditions" (Ph.D. dissertation, University of Wisconsin, Madison, 1981); Kathleen M. Puhr's "Novelistic Responses to the Vietnam War" (Ph.D. dissertation, St. Louis University, 1982); Philip D. Beidler's *American Literature and the Experience of Vietnam* (University of Georgia Press, 1982); and John Hellman's *American Myth and the Legacy of Vietnam* (Columbia University Press, 1986). Discussing the works of Gene Moore, John Briley, James Webb, Gustav Hasford, David Halberstam, Daniel Ford, Tim O'Brien, and Victor Kolpacoff, Stewart sees four basic subjects in the fiction: (1) the contest between civilization and savagery; (2) war as an honorable male initiation; (3) war as a job to be done; and (4) the contest between mind and matter. As does much of the serious criticism, Stewart's work attempts to place selected Vietnam novels into the tradition of previous American war literature.

A different approach is taken by Kathleen Puhr who groups thirty-seven novels by approximate internal chronology and discusses them in both literary and historical contexts from 1945 to 1975. She then selects five novels to examine for their expressions of political propaganda, realism, a "blend of realism and absurdism," "pure absurdism," and documentary fiction (p. 187). Finally, she writes about Tim O'Brien's two books, *If I Die in a Combat Zone* and *Going After Cacciato* in terms of O'Brien's ability to show the truth about Vietnam by means of both fact and fiction.

Finally, Peter Leonard Stromberg's Cornell dissertation (1974), *A Long War's Writing: American Novels About the Fighting in Vietnam Written While Americans Fought*, should be noted as the first lengthy piece of criticism done on the literature of the war. Now superseded because of the numbers of novels published since 1973, Stromberg's work is nevertheless valuable for the views of a professional soldier/scholar in the early 1970s. The best annotated bibliography is John Newman's *Vietnam War Literature* (Scarecrow, 1982).

Most insightful and comprehensive, however, is Philip Beidler's recent book, *American Literature and the Experience of Vietnam*. Showing that much Vietnam fiction does indeed echo the Leatherstocking/Deerslayer/Natty Bumppo frontier myth, Beidler nevertheless manages to identify particular qualities of Vietnam War novels that show how Vietnam "became its own bizarre, hermetic mythology" (p. 13). Beidler notes "the silent, suffocating truth that [Vietnam] was surely enough the biggest game there was: cowboys versus gooks, played in every moment for terrible stakes, and for reasons no one would ever be able to explain" (p. 15). Sounding much like Norman Mailer in *Why Are We in Vietnam?* (1967), Beidler shows how the fiction of America's latest war derives from and contains the attitudes of the past: "The experience of the war similarly and equally has its prophecy . . . in the gliding, shadowed forms of an unseen enemy, the wily inscrutable foe, the spectres of the forest, the multitudinous host born of a whole Western world's best demonological imaginings" (p. 22).

Although focusing on only a few works, John Hellman's *American Myth and the Legacy of Vietnam* shows how ten novels, seven works of nonfiction, and three films allow one to see that "the essence of the American error in Vietnam" was to make "a momentous decision on the basis simply of right intention and past luck" (p. 216). Using an interdisciplinary approach, Hellman demonstrates how not only the myth of the American frontier hero but also that of the hard-boiled detective problem solver became subverted by Vietnam. What we should realize, Hellman asserts, is that "the American Adam . . . is not an exception to history and the fallen world of time, but is rather a limited, fallible person whose destiny is in profound doubt" (p. 217).

These analyses by Stromberg, Beidler, Stewart, Hellman, and Puhr seem to me to be the best, but also valuable are the dissertation by Mardena Creek and earlier articles by Tobey C. Herzog, Larry Van Dyne, and Perry Dean Young. Not to be overlooked, either, is the first significant piece of scholarly criticism done on Vietnam War fiction, Wayne Miller's 1972 Modern Language Association oral paper entitled "Southeast Asia, The War in Fiction" (in manuscript). Miller believed then that only Kolpacoff's *The Prisoners of Quai Dong*, Halberstam's *One Very Hot Day*, my own *Laotian Fragments*, and James Crumley's *One to Count Cadence* deserved "serious consideration as literature" (p. 2). "It may not please many of us," Miller concludes prophetically, "that of the ideologically-oriented works most are right wing rather than liberal or leftist. That is the way it is, however, and in some small way, that fact may be an indication of the direction in which the culture is headed" (p. 16).

This relatively sparse body of criticism written about the literature of the Vietnam War certainly does illuminate the works themselves and also begins to place the novels into a wider context: the tradition of American literature itself. Puhr and Beidler use what I think to be the most success-ful approach: that of discussing the works chronologically by approximate date of internal action. Beidler also carefully blends his discussion of fiction with the "factual" works of a given period, thus providing a finely tuned comparison between the fictions and their contexts as reported in memoirs and autobiographical writings.

Accordingly, I too should like to proceed chronologically through the novels of the Vietnam War, and also to repeat the warnings of both Puhr and Beidler about the need to note the dates. As *Moby-Dick* is not only about an earlier whaling industry but also about the decline of religion and capitalism as Melville saw these institutions *in his own time*, so are most of the Vietnam novels reflective not only of the time periods in which they are set but also of the times in which they were written. Thus, even though the events of Robin Moore's *Green Berets* and Jonathan Rubin's *The Barking Deer* show similar characters in action at nearly the same place and time (1964—the Vietnam highlands), it would be simplistic, I think, to account for the differences in the visions of the two authors merely by noting that Moore is a hawk and that Rubin obviously is a dove. More indicative, I believe, are the dates of writing and publication: *Green Berets* in 1965; *The Barking Deer* in 1974. If Rubin would have written his work in 1965 (and I do not know when he started it), *The Barking Deer* certainly could not have been immediately published, so favorable was the mood of the country in 1966 toward our cause in Vietnam. Many other works reflect the same kind of split perception: the author's vision while writing versus the actuality of his view while experiencing Vietnam. Consequently, a reader of Vietnam fiction should establish two frames of reference when approaching a Vietnam novel: first, the approximate place and time period of the book's internal action; and second, an *external* frame of reference that includes a knowledge of the basic historical events plus the book's date of writing and publication. Only then, I suspect, can a reader appreciate the maximum relevance of any given work.

So—what follows is an attempt to provide an overview of selected Vietnam fiction in order to examine the war through the eyes of literary artists, those men and women who differ from reporters, political analysts, and historians because as writers of fiction their visions usually encompass not only "the way it was" to them but also the way it *should be* to every one else as well. I will discuss the novels in approximate chronological order established by internal reference to attempt to show not only how the Vietnam war evolved but also how the changing attitudes toward the war become so well reflected by the artists themselves.

To provide an overall structure, I suggest that the Vietnam War be viewed as a standard Shakespearean tragedy, in five acts, with a prologue and a rather ragged epilogue (these are the divisions I use in *Vietnam Voices*):

Prologue: to 1955, the formation of the Viet Minh to the accession of Ngo
  Dinh Diem as "Chief of State" of South Vietnam.
Act I: to 1963, the assassination of John F. Kennedy and the murder of
  Diem.
Act II: to January 1968, the American buildup and the North Vietnamese-
  Vietcong Tet offensive.
Act III: to May 1970, the beginnings of the Nixon withdrawal program to
  the invasion of Cambodia and the deaths at Kent State.
Act IV: to January 1973, the "Vietnamization" of the war to the "peace"
  agreement.
Act V: to 30 April 1975, the growing demoralization of South Vietnam to
  the abrupt fall of Saigon.
Epilogue: everything since 1975.

Such a structure at least makes possible an overview of the war, but one should also be aware that in this five-act drama there are multiple scenes that will often show extremely different wars in progress at the same time. Each time period and each geographical setting (even down to a particular province of Vietnam) afforded the American cast a unique experience, so that a novel set in Laos in 1969, for instance, often seems to present a much different war than does another novel about the marines in I Corps or one about the army in the Delta during the same time period. Finally, one must realize that despite the chronological and geographical differences in the settings and action of the works themselves, the "Vietnam" War actually took place in five contiguous Southeast Asian countries: China, Laos, Thailand, and Cambodia, as well as Vietnam itself.

Prologue   to 26 October 1955

Major General (then Colonel) Edward Geary Lansdale, whose autobiography *In The Midst of Wars* (1972) presents a sanitized but fascinating story of his work for the CIA in Saigon from 1953 onward, is the model for a major character in at least three novels: Graham Greene's *The Quiet American* (1955); Eugene Burdick and William Lederer's *The Ugly American* (1958); and Jean Larteguy's *Yellow Fever* (1965). Graham Greene knew of Lansdale in Saigon during 1954, as the colonel was commanding the top-secret Saigon Military Mission (SMM), and even though the events of *The Quiet American* are set in 1951 and 1952, Alden Pyle, the American who is working quietly for the CIA, is unmistakably modeled on Lansdale* (his dog, for instance, was named "Duke," as is Pyle's). Also clear is Greene's opinion of this American who is attempting to establish a "Third Force" among the right- and left-wing Vietnamese factions, neither of whom care for the French. To *The Quiet American*'s narrator, Fowler, Pyle has "the caution of a hero in a boy's adventure story. . . . quite unaware of the absurdity and improbability of his adventure" (p. 145). When Pyle is murdered because he has become too "involved," Greene shows a senior American official viewing the events around him with "pained perplexity: an eternal brother who didn't understand" (p. 32).

Similarly, in *The Ugly American* Lansdale is caricatured as Colonel Hillandale, the "Six-foot Swami" who has studied astrology and palmistry in order to better ingratiate himself as a military adviser to the "Sarkanese." Only one of the inept, shortsighted Americans in this novel, Colonel Hillandale and others like him remain behind when U.S. Ambassador MacWhite is recalled for publicly stating that "the Vietnamese, both Communist and anti-Communist, hated the French. . . . [and] that the French hoodwinked the American military into thinking everything was rosy" (pp. 221–22).

In a third novel, *Yellow Fever* (1965) by Jean Larteguy, Lansdale appears as Colonel Teryman (*terre* = land), who is represented by the Americans as "a new Lawrence of Arabia" (p. 199). Larteguy's fiction is thinly disguised fact, and with Colonel Teryman at the right hand of the soon-to-be president of Vietnam, *Yellow Fever* chronicles the evacuation of Hanoi after the peace agreement, the battles between the factions in the South, and the events of 1954–55 that led to the assumption of power (with U.S. direction) of Ngo Dinh Diem. Throughout, Colonel Teryman is shown to be an eager, unwitting but powerful dupe of the Vietnamese power structure, and his championing (as did Pyle in *The Quiet American*) of a moderate "third force" leader (General Thé) proves ineffectual when Teryman's and Pyle's favorite general is assassinated. At the novel's end in 1956, Colonel Teryman is back in favor with the newly "elected" president and, according to a French journalist in Saigon, "is bored stiff because he can't find anyone 'suitable' to put up against [Diem]. So he spends his time planning

---

*Peter Stromberg disagrees (p. 32); Lansdale believes he was the model.

referendums, rigged elections and agrarian reform, which will put the whole country up in arms" (p. 378). Although the Americans, Larteguy concludes, do hope to establish a "little Republic," their main concern is how much it will cost.

That these three novels each show eager, unsophisticated Americans in an environment that they can neither understand nor completely control becomes ironic when one notes that these early authors were British, American, and French, thus giving an international flavor to the initial fictional castigation of Americans at war in Vietnam. Much the same view also appears in Robert Shaplen's *A Forest of Tigers* (1956), which is set in 1954 as the Geneva peace talks are in progress.

With the "temporary" partitioning of Vietnam in 1954, both regimes allowed inhabitants to migrate to the other. M. J. Bosse's *The Journey of Tao Kim Nam* (1959) presents a sympathetic, detailed portrait of a young North Vietnamese man who reluctantly decides to leave his home in the north and move south. He senses the loss of individuality and freedom as the new North Vietnamese commissars begin to organize his village, but on the voyage to Saigon in a U.S. ship, and especially when he arrives in Saigon, Tao Kim Nam finds squalor, dishonesty, and danger in his newly chosen world. On shipboard, for instance, the elder Vietnamese refuse to take action to stop a black market operation, believing that the best recourse is to "wait for the Americans to punish them, [to] let the army men have what they want, because they won't have it long; the Americans will punish them." At the end, in a refugee camp near Saigon, Tao is certain of only one fact, the noon sun. "It was a hard Asian sun, what his father used to tell him was the only thing in life a man could be sure of—the sun came, the sun went away, the sun came again. The sun was the Viet's only gift" (p. 283).

Act I 1955 to November 1963, the Presidency of Ngo Dinh Diem

At this point I should note one characteristic of Vietnam War fiction: a large number of the novels have as their crisis actions the events of a major political, social, or military upheaval. The four novels already mentioned emphasize the 1954 peace talks and the bloody accession of Diem; later novels will cluster around the 1963 assassinations, the Tet offensive, the effect of the Cambodian invasion, and the fall of Saigon. Few Vietnam novels are truly timeless, yet, as I will point out, two of those that cannot be chronologically dated are among the most successful literary accomplishments.

There is no significant fiction that depicts the slow, covert American aid buildup after the 1954 Geneva agreements. Instead, writers turned to Laos during the late Eisenhower and early Kennedy period. In his stories "The Ambush" and "The French Lesson," as well as in his novel *The Land of a Million Elephants* (1970), Asa Baber portrays first some episodes of the U.S. "White Star" military training teams covertly placed in Laos, then, in his remarkable novel, presents the black comedy of Chanda (Laos) during late 1960 as U.S.- and Soviet-backed factions struggled for power. One of the many novels that does not conclude but slides into the fabulous, *The Land of a Million Elephants* shows that the "reality" of war in Southeast Asia has itself become surreal, and the people of this little country can survive only by reverting to folk magic to deter the intrusions of the superpowers.

Also set in Laos during the early sixties are portions of two other novels, Pamela Sanders's *Miranda* (1978) and Thomas Fleming's unfortunately titled *Officers' Wives* (1981). In Sanders's novel, Miranda Pickerel is a *Time* stringer who travels between Vientiane, Phnom Penh, and Saigon, and her satiric portraits of the CIA in Laos and of the media and military in Saigon show a perceptive reporter's vision. When Miranda visits a recently established Special Forces camp, however, she meets American soldiers who are motivated and dedicated, and Sanders's attitude seems to be that the American presence in the field (if not in the urban headquarters) is well-intended and positive, even with interservice rivalry and expected military snafus. Similarly, in *Officers' Wives*, the most ambitious historical novel of the war, the Americans who advise the Lao and the South Vietnamese are dedicated and honorable. Their problems in 1961–62 result from the incompetence and corruption of their Asian counterparts.

By the end of 1962, 11,300 U.S. servicemen were "officially" stationed in Vietnam (published government figures never include CIA or USAID), and the war still consisted primarily of small actions by both sides. As did Asa Baber, James Crumley served in Southeast Asia, and his novel *One To Count Cadence* (1969) shows the earliest major combat scene between an American unit and the enemy. Sergeant Slag Krummel, who claims when drunk to be "the last survivor of an Apache attack on Fort Dodge, Iowa" (p. 53), is an American bred to be a warrior, a fighter, a brawler, and he considers war to be "the last noble thing" (p. 149). In 1962 his communications unit is sent to Vietnam at night in civilian clothes, encounters ambushes and booby traps, takes casualties, conducts itself well, and wins a pitched battle against the Viet Cong. At the novel's end, Krummel is just back from Laos and a job with CIA. Like Mailer's *Naked and the Dead*, with which *One to Count Cadence* has been compared, this novel presents Americans whose current war just happens to be in Vietnam, and there are no political overtones at all. Also set during this period is Peter Derrig's *The Pride of the Green Berets* (1966), in which all the standard elements of an action-filled war novel are present: a Special Forces team that survives against odds, an heroic, knife-wielding colonel, a love affair with a Vietnamese woman, and other assorted clichés—all this despite good and bad Americans and allies.

Set at almost the same time, David Halberstam's *One Very Hot Day* (1967) is second only, I think, to Graham Greene's *The Quiet American* in its depiction of the distance between the Americans' understanding of Vietnam and the reality that exists there. American Captain Beaupre is an experienced, Vietnamese-speaking adviser to a Vietnamese unit commanded by Captain Thuong, who has already had five American advisers. This novel, whose time-span is only one day, explores the inability of the Americans to influence the basic tactics and thinking of the Vietnamese, with the result that at the climactic battle (no doubt modeled on the debacle of Ap Bac in December 1962), the South Vietnamese are defeated, some Americans are killed, and as Beaupre, "a short hulk of a man carrying an immense load," reflects as he walks down the road, the result of all his efforts has been that "the VC were getting close" (p. 216).

Shortly afterward, as President Diem experienced increasing opposition from his own generals, and as both the North Vietnamese and the Americans increased their efforts, the events of 1963 inspired a number of novels and stories. Charles Larsen's *The Chinese Game* (1969), Smith Hempstone's *A Tract of Time* (1966), Robert Vaughn's *The Valkyrie Mandate* (1974), and Morris West's *The Ambassador* (1965) are all concerned with the generals' coup against Diem. Larsen depicts American army advisers becoming involved with Vietnamese factional politics; Hempstone describes the problems faced by a CIA adviser to a Montagnard tribe as Vietnamese groups jockey for power; Vaughn has his protagonist, Vietnamese-speaking Lt. Colonel Justin Barclay, become actively involved with the conspirators; and West portrays the agonies of the American ambassador (based on Henry Cabot Lodge) as he condones the coup against the president of

Vietnam. From differing perspectives, each of these novels shows the growing inability of the South Vietnamese to maintain internal unity, the increasing threat from the Viet Cong and North Vietnamese, and the prevailing bewilderment of the Americans as they find themselves unable to discover anyone to help further the growth of the "little republic" for which they are fighting. As an American pilot in *The Chinese Game* says, "You know what's wrong with this fouled up hemorrhoid of a war? . . . There's no rutting villains" (p. 186). In each of the novels the major American characters feel guilt and shame for their complicity in helping cause the catastrophes and deaths that have occurred, and as Morris West's American ambassador looks at himself in the mirror after the murder of the Vietnamese president, he sees "the most hateful image" he has ever seen (p. 260).

Fleming's *Officers' Wives* also details the events of the Diem coup, but from the point of view of regular U.S. army officers who have no real knowledge of the plotting. Fleming accurately shows the Americans' confusion about their roles and responsibilities in the "new" Vietnam, and particularly poignant is the scene in late November when the wife of an arrested Vietnamese officer comes to ask one of the American wives for assistance. Referring to the recent assassination of President Kennedy, Thui Dat apologizes:

> "I am ashamed to burden you at such a time. When you are no doubt as shocked by the murder of your president as I was at the death of Diem. Do you think Kennedy was the victim of traitorous Generals in your American Army?"
>
> "No!" Joanna said. "Such a thing is—really quite impossible."
>
> Thui heard the words as a rebuke. She nodded sadly. "You mean such things occur only in wretched countries like Vietnam," she said. "You are no doubt correct." (p. 453).

Act II   1963 to the Tet Offensive, January 1968

Much of the fiction that treats this period of the war shows the transition not only from small-unit action to large-scale military operations but also delineates the authors' progression from optimism through doubt to pessimism over the future of the American effort. Changing too are the attitudes of characters themselves, especially the Americans. (Few of the Western novelists seem to handle Vietnamese characters with much depth.) Although most of the early works do present well-meaning, dedicated

American military men, most of the novels that are set later in the war show increasingly embittered, amoral American servicemen who, like West's ambassador, either quickly become or are already disillusioned by their participation in the war and spend their tours merely trying to survive. Also, as the one-year tour became standard, most of the novels focus on this annual rotation that comes to symbolize the cyclical and unending tragedy of the U.S. involvement in the war.

During 1964 the official number of U.S. servicemen in Vietnam increased from 16,000 to 23,000, but despite growing Viet Cong and North Vietnamese strength, total American combat deaths reached only 267 by December. As one would expect, the U.S. Army Special Forces continued to provide most of the characters for fiction set in the year after Diem's death. Perhaps the best-known book of the war, Robin Moore's *Green Berets* (1965) is a realistic, accurate account of motivated Americans serving their country in a frustrating war. Moore's Americans hardly try to understand their environment or the implications of their presence in Vietnam; instead, they shape Vietnam and Laos to fit their own myths. Their in-country headquarters "looks exactly like a fort out of the old west" (p. 25), and one night the Green Berets show an "epic western" movie for their Vietnamese allies: "The strikers loved the action and identified themselves with it. When the Indians appeared the strikers screamed 'vc,' and when the soldiers or cowboys came to the rescue the Nam Luong irregulars vied with each other in shouting out the number of their own strike-force companies" (p. 127). At the time, it was entirely appropriate that John Wayne was picked to star in the movie version. Moore's message? With proper assistance, there are still "limitless possibilities" in Vietnam.

Apparently equally enthusiastic (but there may be some irony here) is Richard Newhafer's fanciful *No More Bugles in the Sky* (1966). An air force pilot on a secret mission, Dan Belden flies numerous combat sorties (some against the same Chinese pilot he knew in Korea) and succeeds in widening the war enough to allow the U.S. president to send 100,000 more troops to Vietnam, supposedly to get the war won. Also optimistic is Gene D. Moore's *The Killing at Ngo Tho* (1967), whose characters include Vietnamese patriots, loyal professional officers, and capable leaders. When the American-advised Vietnamese find and destroy a hidden Viet Cong headquarters, the novel ends with hope for the future. Similar in outlook is one of the last positive (and actually one of the best) novels set early in the war, Scott C. S. Stone's *The Coasts of War* (1966). A rare navy story, this book shows Lieutenant (SG) Eriksen patiently and understandingly advising a South Vietnamese junk force. When the Viet Cong implant heads of slain villagers on stakes, Lt. Eriksen does likewise with dead VC. As a result, he is reprimanded by his headquarters in Saigon. Despite many problems with American brass and the enemy, Lt. Ericksen does his duty and leaves the Vietnamese junk force in better shape than when he came. Finally, Daniel Ford's realistic novel *Incident at Muc Wa* (1967), although not "optimistic" in the same sense as those just mentioned, shows that a Special Forces operation fails primarily because of the personalities, methods, and politics of the commanders who bicker foolishly and depend upon "Incident-Flow-Priority indicators." Ford shows no sentiment against the war itself, just the way it is being conducted, but in attacking the command and control methodology, Ford's novel becomes prophetic. Another highly sympathetic novel is Thomas Taylor's first Special Forces book *A-18* (1967). In great part a detailed study of Special Forces training and tactics, *A-18* ends with a combat insertion of a Special Forces unit into North Vietnam and shows American fighting men at their best.

One should note that the novels by the two Moores, Newhafer, Ford, Taylor, and Stone were published shortly after the 1964 time period that they cover. Other novels with 1964 settings, however, were published much later, and thus reflect their author's distanced perspective and at the same time show more antagonism toward the Vietnam War itself. The main character of Thomas Taylor's *A Piece of Country* (1970), for instance, is a black Special Forces NCO who, because of his conviction and heroism, does manage to raise the fighting capabilities of his Vietnamese advisees. However, despite Sgt. Taylor's professionalism, the final message of the novel is that if and when the Vietnamese are left on their own, they will be unable to defeat the North Vietnamese and Viet Cong.

Jonathan Rubin's *The Barking Deer* (1974) is a surrealistic parable of the entire Vietnam War, and at the end of this novel about a Special Forces team and Vietnamese tribesmen fighting North Vietnamese regulars and Viet Cong, everyone dies. Why are the Americans there with their electronic sensors and black boxes? Because the North Vietnamese are helping the Viet Cong. And why are the North Vietnamese there? Because the Americans are helping the South Vietnamese. And for whom does the deer (prophesying death) bark? It barks for everyone.

Equally bleak is *Parthian Shot* (1975) by Loyd Little, but this novel's bizarre subject matter shows its intention to be the *Catch-22* of the Vietnam War. At times it almost succeeds, but Little's moralizing blunts the humor. After being declared officially "replaced," a Special Forces unit joins with the North Vietnamese to form a company that makes Viet Cong flags, then sells shares and obtains a Small Business Administration loan. There is a black American who thinks he is Asian and a white soldier who thinks he's black. After one incident in which units from all factions claim to have been attacked by each other, the narrator reflects,

> Somehow it made as much sense as everything else. Or as little. The VC wanted to free the South Vietnamese for the North Vietnamese government, although maybe as a side effect for the South Vietnamese. The KKK [Khmer—Cambodians] wanted to free South Vietnam from Cambodia. The U.S. Army wanted to free the South Vietnamese for the South Vietnamese Government, and maybe, as a side effect, for the South Vietnamese themselves. The Nungs wanted to free something because they were being paid four thousand piastres each a month. And all the South Vietnamese wanted was to grow a little rice (pp. 163–64).

At the end, like the people of *The Barking Deer*, everyone on all sides dies.

An even more recent book set in 1964 is Bo Hathaway's *A World of Hurt* (1981). This novel shows two draftees volunteering for Special Forces and being sent to a base near Nha Trang. During their time in Vietnam they and their "strikers" have numerous firefights with the enemy, but they do not see much hope of eventual victory. After one encounter with an enemy force, during which they have called in U.S. helicopter gunship support, they find only a few burned monkeys, yet they radio the following report: "Roger. You guys did a great job. We got three bunkers and, let's see, five automatic weapons positions destroyed. And . . . they caved in about twenty meters of trench line. . . . We found quite a bit of blood. I'd say they must've had at least six killed. Probably three times that many wounded. Over" (p. 194). The monkeys, meanwhile, have been skinned and prepared for dinner. At the novel's end, Madsen and Sloan are bitter and disillusioned and think only of leaving the army.

One of the more remarkable novels set during this time period is *Into a Black Sun* (1968; trans. 1980) by Japanese correspondent Takeshi Kaiko. With setting and circumstances resembling those of the *Green Berets* (a reporter accompanies a Special Forces unit into combat), this novel probes the philosophy and psychology of West versus East, power, and revolution. Kaiko presents American Captain Wain (one wonders if the translation is an intentional homonym) as a Minnesota farmer possessing "vast reserves of conviction and incorruptibility" (p. 19), then speculates: "Looking at him I thought of the thousands and thousands of hamburgers, tens of thousands of cokes, that had been consumed to form his body" (pp. 8–9). Kaiko offers acute insights into the ruthlessness of the communists and the naive militarism of the Americans; then, during the climactic battle that becomes more and more surreal in its reality, the American advisers are killed, the Vietnamese break and run, and the Japanese narrator flees deeper into the ominous forest. Kaiko's assessment of the American captain's motives seems particularly relevant:

> There was some raw, insatiate energy . . . that drove him on. . . . It made me think of men in covered wagons, those ancestors of his who rode into the great plains and drove the Indians out. Moving, plowing, praying after killing, repenting and moving on, arriving at a goal and, once established, drinking hard and sometimes ending their own lives in violent ways. Men of excess, both heaven- and hell-bent. Wasn't it their strange, restless blood that flowed in him? (pp. 198–99)

In March 1965 the United States publicly committed itself to a military solution, and most of the novels set after this date concern the massive American intrusion that followed the landing of the first two battalions of U.S. Marines at Da Nang. Stationed at that base, Navy Lieutenant Dick Shea watched the marines come ashore. He records his impressions in his book *Vietnam Simply* (1967), a "novel" consisting of linked verse narrative and lyric fictions:

> and so
> en masse
> the marines have landed
> bringing with them
> a high state of nervousness
> and inexperience
> and my little city
> is not itself anymore
>
> .   .   .   .
>
> welcome suckers.

More strident in his antiwar message is William Wilson in his *LBJ Brigade* (1966), a transitional novel that shows a new recruit (the narrator) unable to accept the teachings of the old, wise Sergeant Sace (who speaks French and Vietnamese and is an old Vietnam hand). As a result, the narrator's disobedience causes first Sace's death, then his own. Wilson shows the inhumanity on both sides and severely chastises the American press, while at the same time indicating that the North Vietnamese/Viet Cong tactics are probably better than those of his own forces.

Shea's and Wilson's books are two of the first published antiwar creative works. Other novels written by journalists (Halberstam, Hempstone, Robin Moore, Larteguy) or observing professional novelists (Greene, West, Bosse) had emphasized the naivete and ineptness of the Americans, but in none of these does the sense of impending disaster so overwhelm the reader as in *Vietnam Simply* and the *LBJ Brigade*.

By the end of 1965 there were 184,000 American servicemen in Vietnam, an increase of 161,000 in ten months. No wonder, then, that one of the subjects that pervades the novels set during this period is the relationship between new and old: the earlier conflict versus the newer war; the experienced but war-wise "lifer" NCO versus the new draftee. In these novels the predominant characters are American GIs who arrive in Vietnam only to become quickly appalled at the vestiges of what has been such a long war (the rusting C-ration cans, the battle scars on the landscape, the whorehouses), then quickly learn to play what they see as the only game in town: survival.

Shown by Wilson in *The LBJ Brigade*, this clash of past and present is also at the center of Alan Clark's *The Lion Heart* (1969). Clark's main character is Lt. Jack Lane, one of the many Special Forces officers who is being redeployed with newly arrived main-force units. In Saigon, Lane meets a "real Madison Avenue Colonel" and, in a conversation with a friend, hears that "a lot of the guys that are short are opting out of this one. Going back to the Rock for the last few weeks, and then home." Lane answers, "I've still got six months." His friend replies, "I got four. But it's going to be a ball from now on. We're gonna really *hit* Charlie. I seen the stuff that's coming in" (p. 112). Lane's thoughts, however, reflect upon the French experience; then, the disaster of a subsequent classic military operation and the overall picture of corrupt, inept South Vietnamese show that Clark, despite his overall admiration for the American military man, has severe doubts about the eventual success of the American efforts.

Also set during this period is William Pelfrey's *The Big V* (1972), one of the best realistic novels of the war. The story of Private Henry Winstead, draftee and college graduate, *The Big V* codifies all of the themes, motifs, and subjects that are used in other Vietnam fictions. There is the John Wayne attitude of many Americans, the amazement felt by some who find that the war is so different from what they had seen on television, the sadness at hearing the stewardesses say, "Goodbye—see you in a year," and the pictures of the children selling Coca-Cola and their sisters as Winstead's unit moves into combat. Overall, *The Big V* contains absolutely authentic characters and language. At the death of a soldier whose combat nickname is, symbolically, Anacronism, Private Winstead feels numbed: "All of it, everything I had seen, felt, done; it meant nothing. I had learned that, so why hassle my brain? Yet I knew even then that I would be hassled the rest of my life, like a goddamned movie character" (pp. 157–58). The truncated ending of this novel implies a continuum to follow—that the war will continue without appreciable change.

Also set during 1966–67 is MacAvoy Layne's remarkable poetic novel, *Why Audie Murphy Died in Vietnam* (1973). More sophisticated than Shea's *Vietnam Simply*, Layne's book develops its narrative by also presenting linked lyrics (many of which stand by themselves) to show by a succession of fragments the story of a marine recruit experiencing training, combat, R&R, heroism, capture, and eventual decoration by the president of the United States. Highly realistic at first, *Audie Murphy* explodes into surrealism in its later scenes, and the ironic bitterness of the novel is clear as Murphy declines the Silver Star (the award is being telephoned to him from Washington to his prison in Hanoi):

> And I would like to ask that all the campaign
> Ribbons being worn today be sent to Washington
> To rest.
> And that America become the first civilized country
> Of the world
> to stop the awarding and wearing
> Of
> Commendation
> Medals
> For
> Killing.

Concerning events set at the same time but written from a completely different perspective is Stephen Phillip Smith's *American Boys* (1975), in which there appears a subtheme of sustained admiration for the tenacity of the enemy, the Viet Cong and NVA who face massive American firepower. The main American characters are helicopter crewmen, and after one day-long attempt to kill a lone enemy soldier, a door gunner estimates that the cost for munitions, crew time, helicopters, and aircraft has exceeded $55,000—with B-52 strikes still to come:

> At chow the talk was only of the man. He had earned everyone's respect, was almost a hero, but one who had to be killed. He seemed to excite the imagination like some Jesse James or Billy the Kid whose daring caused envy and admiration in those whose great satisfaction would be to kill him. For Chambers the man assumed heroic proportions. He hoped he was indestructible (p. 357).

The lone VC apparently survives; instead, it is the Americans who are killed or succumb to narcotics and alcoholism.

One of the most mature novels also set in 1966–67 is Winston Groom's *Better Times Than These* (1978). Mixing fact and fiction, using actual dates and locations (the Ia Drang Valley) and also showing attitudes toward the war of civilians at home, Groom presents the story of a company whose representative officers and men (a Jew, an Ivy Leaguer, a congressman's son, and a Mississippi farm boy) find out what the Vietnam War is all about. After a major firefight, Colonel Patch observes the blood trails left by the enemy and would "sure like to know how many of the bastards they took with them," then adds, "We're going to have to make a guess. I don't see a single one" (p. 391). They do, however, discover one VC body attended by a pet monkey, and the message of this novel is much like that of Hathaway's *A World of Hurt* and Smith's *American Boys*: Americans are destroying themselves more than they are the enemy.

Also written shortly after the author's Vietnam experience was John Rowe's *Count Your Dead* (1968), a novel that ranks as one of the most bitter indictments written about the American presence in Vietnam. American and Vietnamese officers and men are seen as incompetent liars as they fumble, inflate enemy casualties, or die. Those who survive are rewarded for their sins.

Another novel set in 1966–67 shows a different and unique perspective. Charles Nelson's *The Boy Who Picked the Bullets Up* (1981) depicts a morphine-addicted homosexual returning to the United States after having served as a navy medic. Strom, the protagonist, alternates between sexual encounters and battle experiences—yet the overall effect is realistic, and sad.

By mid-1967, with over 400,000 soldiers stationed in Vietnam, the Americans seemed to many to have completely taken over the war, the pacification programs, and the country itself. One of the most humorous novels, Derek Maitland's *The Only War We've Got* (1970) satirizes not only the CORDS program for Revolutionary Development, actually run by special ambassador Robert Komer, but also the entire American effort— including "tunnel rats" and war correspondents. The head of CORDS, Ambassador Risher, outlines his new program for winning the war: "In broad terms, we're going to uproot all the people—all sixteen million of them—and resettle them in a heavily-guarded reservation outside Saigon. Then we're gonna defoliate the entire rest of the country and turn it into a free-fire zone, and anyone caught moving out there—v.c. or not—is going to get his ass shot off" (pp. 134–35). Risher's ultimate solution? "The only way we're gonna win this war . . . is to tow the goddam country out into the middle of the Pacific and bomb the shit out of it until it sinks" (p. 135).

Equally satiric, William Eastlake's *The Bamboo Bed* (1969) presents a mad panorama of the scene in 1967 as American Captain Knightbridge fornicates his way around and above the war. Seeing the absurd humor in the growing horror, Eastlake also comments directly on actual figures such as General Westmoreland, whose "light at the end of the tunnel" speech of 21 November is viciously attacked:

> So General Westmoreland got on an airplane with Ambassador Ellsworth Bunker and both of them went back to the United States of America and announced that they were winning the war. That did not help. Hill 904 was still held by the Unfriendlies. Then one fine day Clancy took it. It cost Clancy ninety-four men, but he took it when all had failed. General Westmoreland and Ambassador Bunker came back to Vietnam. Ambassador Bunker went back to doing whatever Ambassadors do who walk a crooked mile to run a crowded country. Westmoreland gave Clancy a medal. (248)

Perhaps the best novel of 1967 action is Larry Heinemann's *Close Quarters* (1977), which shows armored personnel carrier driver PFC Philip Dosier during and after his combat tour in Vietnam. Stylistically superior to most of the other novels, *Close Quarters* shows a young enlistee systematically introduced to the amorality and horror of the war, to drugs, sensation-seeking newsmen, and sex with "Claymore Face," a Vietnamese woman. Raised "on 'the thou-shalt-nots' and willow switches and John Wayne (even before he became a verb), the Iwo Jima bronze and First and Second Samuel" (p. 53), Dosier experiences a major battle (perhaps the most strikingly written combat scene in any Vietnam novel) and returns just before the 1968 Tet offensive. Even though his girl has waited for him and he does not experience a particularly hostile reception at home, Dosier remains obsessed and traumatized by the war.

Other novelists writing about this period use the VC/NVA Tet offensive as crisis actions, obviously seeing this major series of pitched battles as a turning point in the war. Hugh Atkinson's *The Most Savage Animal* (1972), Robert Roth's *Sand in the Wind* (1973), James Trowbridge's *Easy Victories* (1973), John Cassidy's *A Station in the Delta* (1979), Gustav Hasford's *The Short Timers* (1980), and William Ehrhart's *Vietnam-Perkasie* (1983) (which I am including here because it really *is* a novel), all revolve around Tet and show the various perspectives of International Volunteer Services members, marines, CIA agents and operatives, and other American soldiers and officials. So does Fleming's *Officers' Wives*, in a major section of this panoramic novel. Interestingly, one of the main targets of attack in these novels is the American media, from the reporters who scurry up to the top of the Saigon hotel yelling, "Sock it to them. Sock it to the little bastards" (p. 147) in *The Most Savage Animal,* or the marine photo team who wire the hands and feet of massacred bodies together for a picture in *The Short Timers*, to the CIA agent who assaults a newsman in *A Station in the Delta* because he has concentrated on shipboard drug use instead of reporting that the enemy has been defeated. Although the American protagonists of these novels arrive with (and some manage to maintain) a measure of conviction, they are surrounded by characters who are seen as corrupt, self-serving, brutal, or incompetent. Hasford (much like Smith in *American Boys*) does pay tribute to one lone enemy soldier who survives all attempts to kill him, and Ehrhart presents sympathetic yet naive American characters, but the overall impression that these six novels produce is that regardless of what will follow, for all the reasons one can think of, the war has been a mistake and will probably not be won. Ehrhart, in addition, brings the war home when his narrator is treated like a child at home, is jilted by his girl and spurned by his former friends, then resorts to violence and liquor to try to compensate for his despair.

One of the reasons, perhaps, that Tet so affected the American consciousness of both the citizen and the literary artist can be understood by comparing the messages of the novels that concern the events of 1966–68 with that of Barbara Garson's *MacBird* (1967), a 1965 play that became increasingly popular as the war continued. Early in the war, MacBird (Lyndon Johnson) responds violently to the suggestion that the United States is "trying to subdue" Vietnam:

> What crap is this "we're trying to subdue"?
> Since when do we permit an open challenge
> To all the world's security and peace?
> Rip out those Reds! Destroy them, root and branch!
> Deploy whatever force you think we need!
> Eradicate this noxious, spreading weed! (pp. 54–55)

Because of the Tet offensive (and I do not believe it to have been a military defeat for the U.S./SVN forces), the attitude with which Americans had *entered* the buildup of the war during Act II had not produced the "eradication" that had been so complacently expected; therefore, the despair of many Americans became obvious. Regardless of their political or moral convictions before Tet, Americans had rather thought that President Johnson might have been able, after all, to pull it off—in the good old American way.

Act III   from Tet to the Invasion of Cambodia (May 1970)

If one considers Wayne Miller's comment (quoted earlier) that the majority of novels written before 1972 seemed to show "right-wing" tendencies (i.e., favorable attitudes toward the war), one can see from the perspective of 1985 that the balance certainly shifted in the books published *after* 1972 that depict the events up to and including the Tet offensive of January –May 1968. Most of the earlier novelists seemed to want to show that the war was of course terrible, but that success might be possible with proper attitudes and tactics by the South Vietnamese and the Americans.

Then, when the troop increases failed to provide victory, the novels changed emphasis to show the brutality on both sides and the devastating effect on Americans, perhaps in the hope that those novels written while the war was continuing might shock Americans at home into abandoning it (or at least vow never to become involved again). *After* Tet, however, and especially after President Nixon announced "Vietnamization" and the accelerating withdrawal of American troops, most of the Americans who are characterized in fiction already view the war as a tragic status quo— something that has been going on for a long time, something that would probably neither be won nor lost no matter how long the Americans might remain.

As a result, most of the novels set after Tet contain strong themes of the modern American's inability to comprehend reality itself (the war, after all, has been going on for years)—and the disillusion that the novels present seems to be caused less by the war itself but more from the authors' feelings that even though one *should* be able to understand, hence judge, in actuality correct assessment is impossible—by the president down to the new recruit standing guard duty in a well-worn, graffiti-laden bunker. As U.S. troop strength in Vietnam increased (to a peak of 543,400 in April 1969), so did the antiwar protests at home (the number of protestors present for M-Day in Washington on 15 November 1968 almost equaled the number of GIs in Vietnam). Aside from the war itself, and despite the media coverage, many of the novels set in 1968–70 attempt to show that the main problems of their characters lie in separating fact from fiction, illusion from reality.

Accordingly, novels such as *Gangland, The Laotian Fragments, Going After Cacciato, The Lionheads, Meditations in Green, No Bugles No Drums,* and *Fields of Fire* have at their centers, no matter how "realistic" they appear, the inability of Americans to comprehend and understand the Vietnam experience they are able to see with their own eyes. In a way (and sometimes intentionally), these novels tend more to use the war as metaphor—to show that it is the entire American scene that has in fact become "Vietnamized."

Set in early 1968, Josiah Bunting's *The Lionheads* (1972) presents in its opening chapter a marvelous courtly parody of a division headquarters briefing on 12 March 1968, a "formal masculine assembly which meets regularly and according to a fixed protocol to allow [General Lemming] to take counsel of his greater feudatories and his household knights. All here is order, degree, heraldry, pomp, deference" (pp. 3–4). Among items in the daily briefing are the order of battle, combat incidents during the past twenty-four hours, intelligence summaries, and what has become routine for the now entrenched Americans, the latest construction reports:

> Work on the new E.M. center continues. We hope to open the facility within fifteen working days and it will be able to serve 350 troops at once. . . . Ten table-tennis courts. A library of 1500 paperbacks. Six pool tables. Four television sets. Fifteen portable writing cubicles. Five large coffee urns and popcorn machines. Two jukeboxes and a donut dispenser. (p. 10)

Observing all this is newly arrived Private Paul Compella, who is eventually killed despite the technology and "expertise" on his side. The war in *The Lionheads* has become a tool for management experts and career officers who are looking for their next promotion, and even with the presence of extremely dedicated, courageous officers and men, those who survive, says Bunting in his foreword, will "put away their experience." Of those who die, he adds, "many died uncomprehending" (p. ix).

Also underlining misconception and a lack of understanding is Len Giovanetti's emblematic, irrealistic, and didactic novel *The Man Who Won the Medal of Honor* (1973). Awarded the Congressional Medal for a job he did not do, embittered Private David Glass assaults the president, murders an aide, and is sent to prison (where he ironically belongs for having killed Americans in Vietnam). In the same vein, but presented quite differently, is John Briley's *The Traitors* (1969), a long, uneven novel that is really a philosophical polemic. The plot (American defectors working for the North Vietnamese) serves primarily to allow debates about the morality, conduct, and ultimate purpose of the war in an attempt to get below surfaces and discover ultimate right and wrong. Briley obviously believes that the North Vietnamese cause is just, and in his analysis, not only of the war but also of attitudes toward politics and race in the United States, he calls into question many of the prevailing and accepted American cultural and political beliefs.

Also interesting for its descriptions of Hanoi and the North Vietnamese is Charles Collingwood's *The Defector* (1970), a story about reporter Bill Benson on a CIA mission to extract a North Vietnamese official who wants to defect. When the defector is murdered *after* escaping to South Vietnam, Benson is shown to have been party to an aspect of the war about which he has had little understanding.

Set during the spring and summer of 1968, William Turner Huggett's *Body Count* (1973) ranks among the best realistic novels of the war. Huggett takes no political stance; his officers and men fight as best they can in what they see and feel to be an extremely hostile environment. Throughout, Huggett's characters see the vestiges of previous battles such as Khe Sanh and are awed by the continuity of the war. Overall, however, despite the individual heroism of Lieutenant Hawkins and his platoon, the book ends with little hope for long-term success.

More bewildered by the war is Private John Farmer, the protagonist of Joe Haldeman's *War Year* (1972). His name, I suspect, is significant. Never quite comprehending what he is doing or why he is doing it, Farmer runs afoul of his own military brass as well as the enemy and is killed without ever understanding the reasons for what he has been doing.

Also beginning in August 1968 is Jack Fuller's novel *Fragments* (1984), in which the main character arrives in Vietnam and becomes "swept along despite the arguments" (p. 22) and commits what he has been brought up to believe are atrocities, the killing of women and children. One of the narrator's apparent purposes in telling Neumann's story is to understand: "If I could see the fragments, know exactly what had happened to me and why, then when the ghosts whispered to me that it could have been different, I could prove them wrong" (p. 20). Unable to achieve such understanding and unable even to resume what had been a close friendship with a war buddy, Neumann says, "I thought I knew them . . . I loved them. I had done everything I could think of to help them. How could I have been so wrong?" (p. 205). In his search for understanding, the narrator is able only to conclude that "Nothing is simple, nothing is true" (p. 209).

As the Paris Peace talks sputtered publicly along and President Nixon began U.S. troop withdrawals, the sense of overall unreality that many Americans felt toward the Vietnam War increased. For many, what they saw as "real" had become completely surreal, and Tim O'Brien's *Going After Cacciato* (1981) best blends realistic with highly symbolic fiction. (I am placing *Cacciato* here because of its characters' attitudes and because O'Brien, as shown in his excellent 1973 memoir *If I Die In A Combat Zone*, served in Vietnam from January–December 1969.) Army PFC Paul Berlin's goal in Vietnam is simply "to live long enough to establish goals worth living longer for" (p. 27). While ostensibly tracking their AWOL buddy Cacciato to Paris, Berlin and his friends encounter a VC major to whom they address questions about VC methods and motives with the intention of finding out why and how their enemy has been so successful and enduring. To Li Van Hgoc, the answer is quite simple. For the

Americans, "the land is your enemy" (p. 88). Moral, questing, optimistic, PFC Berlin keeps after his elusive quarry in this novel that should properly be read on one level as an allegory of the entire war itself. Near the end, when Paul Berlin and Sarkin Aung Wan conduct their own "peace talks" in Paris, O'Brien's intent becomes clear. With each man outlining his understandable and defensible attitude toward the war, the talks end without "negotiation. There is only the statement of positions" (p. 323). One man's fact is another's fiction—and as the novel closes, the fact, the fiction, the future, and even imagination itself have become indistinguishable from each other—and only what *might* have been really survives.

For David Winn, too, what is "real" in Vietnam also becomes surreal. His novel *Gangland* (1982) moves back and forth from Private Dunkle's training accident in 1967, his brief tour in Vietnam in early 1969, to his experiences in California during 1975 where, quite appropriately for Winn's dazzling fusion of structure, style, symbol, and theme, Dunkle watches the fall of Saigon on television. Much like those in Ted Mooney's *Easy Travel to Other Planets* (1981), Winn's characters live in a world where information and technology rule and bewilder—and the Vietnam War, "The Greatest Adventure of our Generation" (p. 101) with its electronic weaponry controlled by the master computer ANIMA, is seen as but one example of a modern world gone mad. Dunkle's credo for survival echoes those of many other characters in the later Vietnam fiction: "Admit that things are bad, that they're not going to get any better, and if they *do* change, it'll probably be for the worse, so the best thing to do is mind your own business as best you can" (p. 221). The last scene shows Dunkle acting much like a modern Candide, but instead of gardens, Dunkle's place to work with his hands is a rooftop.

More realistic but no less surreal is Charles Durden's *No Bugles No Drums* (1976), in which American soldiers tend the Song My swine farm and try to stay alive. Written entirely in GI vernacular (many characters are the products of "McNamara's 100,000 . . . pulled from the compost heap of America's hopeless" [p. 43]), this novel depicts drug smuggling in body bags, a pattern of continuing acts of self-preservation, and only momentary sadness when a friend is killed. Sergeant Hawkins is recommended for medals and promotion at the same time he is being charged in a general courts-martial, with the result that "the only thing Subject Hawkins had left was his unshakeable bad attitude" (p. 287). Most revealing, however, is the image that Durden's GIs have of themselves in 1968–69:

We were a pain in the ass, and just as many numbers on some dude's board in Saigon, the Pentagon, and the international desks of the networks. Once a week the voice, for thirty seconds, became somber and the announcements seeped into the ether: Forty-five Americans were reported killed in Vietnam this week. The Dow Jones Industrial average was off today, down three points to 983. No one loved us for bein' their clay 'n' spirit. They were grateful to those of us who went away quietly, without makin' too big a fuss 'r screamin Hell no, we won't go. (pp. 142–143)

Showing events that begin later in 1969 is Donald E. McQuinn's novel, *Targets* (1981). Major Charles Taylor, a military intelligence officer, lands in Saigon and is immediately brought up to date by his new commanding officer, Colonel Winter: "Here it is August '69 and we're still fighting a war that should've been over in '65. In fact, a war that shouldn't have gotten off the ground" (p. 19). Later, a young lieutenant asks Taylor, "What're they saying about the war back home?" Taylor replies, "In terms of popularity, it's somewhere below syphilis. No one seems to understand it. It's killing our people" (p. 33). In a novel that has some of the most sympathetically presented and developed Vietnamese characters of any book written by Americans, McQuinn deftly handles subjects such as the returned veteran, the Vietnamese-American relationship, the morality of war, old guys versus new guys, and the growing impossibility of victory for South Vietnam. At a 1970 departure ceremony for some American officers who are leaving Vietnam, Vietnamese Colonel Loc says, "I think my country is doomed. . . . Once you have all gone home, I think we will be overrun. . . . Your country has tried very hard and honorably to help us become a nation. . . . We have taken the worst of your culture and grafted it into the worst of our culture. It is a sickly plant" (p. 497).

Also featuring an Army intelligence analyst in 1969 is Steven Wright's *Meditations in Green* (1983), a novel that blends fact with fiction in scenes that are alternately real and surreal. With his highly sophisticated techniques (multiple points of view, cinematic cuts, and linked image clusters), Wright represents the growing number of Vietnam authors whose tours in Vietnam were followed by years of graduate school in writing. Similar to, but less jarring than those of *Gangland* and *Cacciato*, Wright's characters, who include "Weird" Wendell who is filming a cinema verité of the war while reading *Atlas Shrugged* and tearing out the pages, and black soldiers who have put their "voodoo hootch" off-limits to whites, all end up dead or addicted to drugs (unlike those of earlier novels, however, many of Wright's characters seem to be steady drug users *before* coming to Vietnam). For Staff Sergeant Griffin, the Vietnam War assumes its own reality: "Each time he witnessed another raw incident like tonight's (the bodies by the road, the ragged line of blindfolded wounded prisoners shuffling from truck to cell) his past took on more and more of the insubstantial character- istics of fantasy. The war was real; he was not" (p. 193).

Also having difficulty separating fact from fantasy are the characters in my *Laotian Fragments* (1974, 1985), a hyper-realistic documentary novel set during late 1969 and early 1970. Each character, whether a CIA agent, an air force pilot, a U.S. Senator, or the fictional editor himself, is seen searching to find out exactly what is going on in the Laotian theater of the overall Vietnam War. None succeeds, and as the main character Major Blake becomes more and more aware of the madness that is controlling the war, he decides to show that one individual can at least make *some* difference. As a result, he is shot down and becomes missing in action. Ironically similar to the message of Jack Fuller's *Fragments*, *The Laotian Fragments* ends with the naive editor *still* not understanding what has transpired in the war, even though he can announce from his scholar's viewpoint that "it is only, I am beginning to suspect, by admitting our inescapable depen- dence on all known elements of the external world that we are led to what we think we know as truth" (p. 240). Sadly, this well-meaning truth seeker has ignored one fragment he has so meticulously edited, where Major Blake, reacting to the explosion of information that is available about the war, says, "Perhaps the real tragedy of today is that we mistake bits and pieces for fact. Too much information—thus, massive ignorance. But we have to make decisions anyway. So what do we do? Flip coins. Roll dice. Guess. Ignorance breeding impulse: what grand ingredients for truth" (p. 188).

Finally for this section, Act III (1968–70), I wish to comment on James Webb's *Fields of Fire* (1978) for two reasons: first, because it is one of the few novels that moves realistically from the home scene (1968–69) to Vietnam and back home again (1970), and second, because I think that it has been misunderstood, much like the Vietnam War itself, by many readers who seem to have applied their own politics to this very important novel. Like Webb's *A Sense of Honor* (1981) (in which there is a character unfortunately named "mad Pratt" who keeps on saying "We're winning in Vietnam" [39]), *Fields of Fire* is really about the inability of Americans of all points of view to discover truth. Almost the only survivor of a platoon that has become bonded together by war and defeated not only by the enemy but also by its own military heritage and tactics as well, wounded veteran Will Goodrich offends a group of Harvard protestors who are chanting "Ho Chi Minh is Gonna Win" by asking them, "LOOK. WHAT DO ANY OF YOU EVEN KNOW ABOUT IT?" (p. 339). Earlier, just before reluctantly agreeing to speak at a rally organized to protest the invasion of Cambodia, Goodrich has said, "I don't know anything about My Lai. But it's a bunch of shit to say it's regular or even condoned. Look, man, I fought with myself about this for *months*. I even turned a guy in for murder. I thought it was my duty. But I just *don't know anymore*" (p. 406). Like most of the novels written about the 1968–70 period of the war, *Fields of Fire* shows that despite one's own experience and despite all of the information that has been put out by all concerned, the truth of the Vietnam War has still eluded everyone.

President Nixon's decision to authorize the invasion of Cambodia on 30 April 1970 sparked massive demonstrations that led to the killing of four students at Kent State University. *Fields of Fire* contains a section about Lam Son 719 told from a Vietnamese soldier's point of view; Michael Rossman's story "The Day We Named Our Child We Had Fish for Dinner" in *Writing Under Fire* (1978) shows the effect of Kent State on a Berkeley couple; and Robert Perea's fine story "Small Arms Fire" in *Cuentos Chicanos* (1980) concerns some GIs observing the massive troop movements toward Cambodia. Otherwise, Lam Son 719 and Kent State do not show up in much other fiction, perhaps because these events themselves seemed themselves so unreal and so illogical that for authors to treat them in fiction might well be compounding the already unbelievable mistake.

Regardless, the novelists who chose to concentrate on this pivotal period of the war, 1968–70, seem to me to have produced a body of work that, together, should rank at the top of anyone's list.

Act IV   from May 1970 to the Peace Treaty, January 1973

The war, of course, continued, but in 1970 some 140,600 American troops were withdrawn, leaving by December a total of 334,600 in country. Compared with what has been written about the previous two and one-half years, the amount of fiction set during the next thirty months seems miniscule—but there are some extremely important works. Five novels,

James Kirkwood's *Some Kind of Hero* (1975), Jim Morris's *Strawberry Soldier* (1972), Allston James's *Attic Light* (1979), Charles Coleman's *Sergeant Back Again* (1980), and Corrine Browne's *Body Shop* (1973) concern physically and emotionally wounded veterans either undergoing treatment at various hospitals and/or experiencing varied problems (including criminal acts) adjusting to civilian life. What predominates in these novels is each author's sincere attempt to show the plight of many Vietnam veterans who were even more ignored as the war, officially, was winding down in the minds of Americans. Usually addicted to drugs, these wounded veterans in the five novels show maladjustments ranging from psychosis to criminality in a society that has not only spurned them but has changed so much that they hardly recognize it. Reading these novels makes one recall Winn's *Gangland*, in which the expressionistic Colonel Boyline says to Dunkle upon his return, "You already feel like you don't belong, like you'll never fit in. . . . You don't have any idea what's going on out there. . . . They [the Americans] eat strange food and drink strange liquor. It's all changed and there's no hope of ever going back or catching up" (p. 149).

Equally troubled but more representative of the new American society are the characters of Robert Stone's *Dog Soldiers* (1974), a novel that begins in Vietnam but then traces the efforts of a veteran and his friends to recover and sell a large amount of drugs sent from Saigon. Set "eight years since Vietnam Day" in Berkeley (1967), Stone's novel, much like Winn's *Gangland*, shows how the absolute absence of values in Vietnam is no different from the situation that exists at home. Carrying the dope that has caused violence and death, Hicks emulates his model Neal Cassady and dies counting railroad ties, and Converse expresses what Stone appears to believe is society's bottom line: "We can't stay and grieve or we'll be just as dead as he is. . . . In the worst of times . . . there's something" (p. 333).

The only major published novel set in Vietnam during 1970–73 (there are some good unpublished works, however, as well as Jerome Doolittle's *The Bombing Officer* [1982], whose setting is Laos) is John Del Vecchio's *The Thirteenth Valley* (1982). It is, as if such an accomplishment were possible, *The Naked and the Dead* about Vietnam. Using techniques that range from the interior monologue to the collage, Del Vecchio skillfully weaves fact and fiction to show how a carefully selected cross section of

American GIs experience, learn from, and do their duty in the waning years of the war. Del Vecchio's sympathetically presented characters have been called stock, but they do represent most of the Americans who experienced Vietnam, and his use of actual action reports, letters, and diary entries gives an air of verisimilitude. *The Thirteenth Valley* is, however, a traditional war novel about men in combat and shows, I think, that Del Vecchio sees the Vietnam War much as earlier authors such as Remarque, Dos Passos, Mailer, and Jones viewed World Wars I and II: war is brutal, dehumanizing, and horrible, but men must do their duty, even though many will die.

Perhaps the most sensitive fiction set during this last period of official American involvement has been written by Walter McDonald, whose novel, "Waiting for the End," has yet to find a publisher. Most of the chapters, however, have been published as short stories in such publications as *Descant*, the *Sam Houston Literary Review*, and *Quartet*. The main character, Liebowitz, is a pilot assigned to Vietnam in 1971–72, and the action of the novel shows his arrival, his attempts to remain humane in face of what he sees as madness, and his eventual shoot-down and return to Japan on a Medevac aircraft. Of particular value is the chapter entitled "The Track," in which American officers doing their daily jogging routine in April 1972 (when there were fewer than 75,000 Americans remaining in Vietnam) hear the "rumble and thunder" as the North Vietnamese unleash their 1972 Easter offensive.

Act V: January 1973 to 30 April 1975

With the American military presence officially ended after January of 1973 (still in country were 7,700 admitted DOD "civilians" in technical and advisory positions, plus a large contingent of U.S. military in Thailand), it is not surprising that most of the fiction derives from the precipitous evacuation of Saigon in April 1975.

One novel, however, is unique. John Balaban's *Coming Down Again* (1985), with action set in 1974 Thailand after the cease-fire, is billed as a "thriller," but it is much more than that. The plot is obviously one that was acceptable to the publisher: an American, Paul Roberts, is in a Thai prison for drug smuggling; "John Lacey, Roberts's buddy, and his band of AWOL soldiers and mercenaries set out to rescue them from their prison hellhole" (proof, flyleaf). This novel, however, contains the most accurate, detailed descriptions ever written about what being in Southeast Asia *felt* to a *farang* (a Western foreigner), and it is Balaban's poet's sensibility that makes the novel, despite its structural flaws, work. For instance, the American prisoner, Roberts, listens to an Asian rain: "The rain's roar was deafening: a fierce tympanic assault of gutter gurgle, leaf splatter, metallic plunks, and the sizzling sweeps of rainsheets hissing through the upper branches of the forest and tearing across the thatched roofs and the muddy prison yard with its dripping mounted mortar" (p. 25). Roberts, like Balaban himself, is a former International Volunteer Service's worker, and when the rescue is successful, Lacey enjoys the feel of the sun "and the bounce of the waves against the bow" of his ship, and Roberts will no doubt "be on a talk show" (p. 238).

The other fictions depict the decline and fall of South Vietnam. Two of Robert Olen Butler's novels, *The Alleys of Eden* (1981) and *On Distant Ground* (1985) show scenes of the Saigon evacuation. *Alleys of Eden* concerns an army deserter fleeing but managing to get his Vietnamese girlfriend as well out of Vietnam. Their life together in the United States is short, however, because the woman leaves the American to join a group of Vietnamese refugees. *On Distant Ground* is the story of Captain David Fleming, convicted of collaborating with the enemy in Vietnam, who returns to Saigon during the evacuation to retrieve his son by his former Vietnamese mistress. Both novels are fast-paced and facile, and the scenes in Vietnam are convincing because of Butler's knowledge of the language and terrain.

Also concerned with the last days of Saigon is Joan Didion's *Democracy* (1984), one of her many postmodernist novels about life in the world today. The main character, Inez Victor, has had a long-standing affair with Jack Lovett, apparently a CIA agent who has been in and out of Vietnam. Lovett manages to get Inez Victor's daughter out of Saigon just as the city falls to the communists, but neither the narrator nor Inez Victor herself ever understands the meaning of all the events, or even exactly who Jack Lovett really was.

The two most convincing novels about the fall of Saigon are Stephen Harper's *Live Till Tomorrow* (1977) and Bernard and Marvin Kalb's *The Last Ambassador* (1981). All three authors were journalists, and each novel shows the tragedy of the effects of the American abandonment of what had been a twenty-year commitment. The Kalbs' novel (an ironic return to the setting of West's *The Ambassador*) shows the last American ambassador to

Saigon caught in the middle between a hostile State Department and a desperate South Vietnamese president, while Harper's *Live Till Tomorrow* depicts the escape of Washington Barber, a former member of the 173rd Airborne division, with the Vietnamese family of his business associate. As were the early novels written by journalists such as Green and Larteguy, these last two books are accurate, compelling, and direct. On board a U.S. Navy aircraft carrier standing off Vung Tau, Washington Barber is asked by a teenaged marine,

> "How was it in Saigon?"
> Barber froze. Saigon had slipped completely from his mind, already like something in the distant past, something better not to think about.
> His jaw tightened as he fought to maintain control over a sudden instinct to cry.
> His voice came taut and unnatural.
> "Kinda nasty."
> The marine sensed Barber's agony.
> "Anyway, it's all over now, I guess." (p. 103)

Epilogue   after 30 April 1975 (and two unclassifiable works)

The occupation of Saigon by the North Vietnamese officially ended the internal aspects of the wars in Laos, Cambodia, and Vietnam, but fighting, of course, continued, especially in Cambodia. So has the writing of fiction set in Southeast Asia, but with notable changes. Joe Haldeman's *The Forever War* (1976) is really an overview, set far in the future, of the effects of a war such as Vietnam on a technologically advanced society. Anyone familiar with Vietnam will see what Haldeman's real subject is. Other novels of varying quality concern Americans who return to Southeast Asia for varying reasons, from Berent Sanford's thrillers, *Brass Diamonds* (1980) and *The Chinese Spur* (1983), to Loyd Little's *In the Village of the Man* (1978). Sanford's two novels (actually the result of a collaboration between Peter Sanford and Mark Berent) benefit from Berent's three tours in Southeast Asia, and Little's novel, set in Laos of 1977, is a sensitive portrayal of an American who finally comes to understand the ways of an ancient Asian people.

Other novels that have been recently proliferating deserve little mention, except to note that the increasing *Gunship* series with its shoot-'em-up distortions not only appeals to the growing American Ramboesque conservatism but may also be extremely damaging to readers who want to find out how Vietnam really was.

Two other novels, however, must be mentioned here, because even though they fit into no particular time period, each is relevant and extremely important. Victor Kolpacoff's *The Prisoners of Quai Dong* (1967) and Ward Just's *Stringer* (1974) seem to me along with Halberstam's *One Very Hot Day* and Kaiko's *Into a Black Sun* to best present the basic problems of Westerners at war in Southeast Asia. Himself a prisoner for refusing to fight, Lieutenant Kreuger in *Quai Dong* is ordered to assist in the interrogation of a captured Viet Cong soldier, and during the course of the novel Kreuger becomes the evil that his side is trying to eradicate. Unable, because of his Western heritage, to see the torture continue, Kreuger lies about what the VC prisoner has told him, inventing the location of the sought-after enemy supply depot. When the friendly troops attack and completely by chance *do* find supplies, Kreuger is released and commended. In this careful psychological study of conflicting values and frames of reference, Kolpacoff (who had never been to Vietnam) shows in a relatively early novel how the Americans can neither comprehend nor positively control the events in Southeast Asia. *The Prisoners of Quai Dong* ends as it began: "Convicts were still scraping the hull of the LST. They were on the port side now. I saw the orderly rows of khaki tents, the guard towers, the spotlights, and the barbed wire. Everything seemed unchanged; the only difference was that I was now standing on the major's porch, instead of on the beach" (p. 213).

Also timeless is Ward Just's *Stringer*, a novel that uses characters from the CIA and the regular army, as well as the existence of American technology, to probe the rationality and purposes of the American presence in a Southeast Asian war. Mixing minute realism with symbolic surrealism, Just presents Stringer (again, particularly because of Just's newspaper background, a significant name) as a CIA operative on his last scheduled mission to plant sensors on enemy infiltration routes. His attitudes are contrasted to those of Price, his regular Army companion who is killed, and the latter part of the novel shows Stringer trying "to separate the parts. . . . To understand the future . . . to understand the past" (p. 195). Stringer's failure to do so synthesizes and epitomizes the dilemma that so pervades the best of the Vietnam novels, especially James Webb's *Fields of Fire*:

anyone who claims to have an inside track on the truth about the Vietnam War is actually demonstrating only biased myopia.

How to conclude what has been at the least an underdeveloped gloss of the writing about Americans during the Vietnam War?

Some patterns emerge: the naiveté of Americans who want to do it all and who become viciously destructive in their attempts; the belief by the Vietnamese that the Americans are all-powerful; the debilitating loss of traditional values *on all sides* as the war escalates; the failure of modern technology to conquer a people who are determined to fulfill what they are told is their destiny; the degrading effect of the war on a proud U.S. military; how the Americans' belief in individuality changes to a sense of being part of an unstoppable, impersonal machine; the overwhelming effect of the Vietnam War on the American scene itself; and the inability, regardless of political, moral, or even religious beliefs, for American novelists to make sense out of the madness that creates wars such as Vietnam in the modern, "civilized" world.

That so many similar conflicts continue unabated in Central America, the Middle East, Africa, and Afghanistan hardly provides any comfort —and when considering these current wars, one should note that in most of the Vietnam novels, the American media does not fare very well as a conduit for "facts." As a shaper of opinion, the media prevails, but most of the novelists include the American press as one of the responsible parties in the overall creation and perpetuation of untruths. Why? In its traditional (some might say naive) belief that the truth *can* be beamed into modern living rooms and understood as such, the media, as represented by most of the Vietnam novelists, may well have fostered rather than resolved the confusion so many readers and viewers have felt.

So, although I admire and commend all those who have written about, reported, recorded, analyzed, and filmed the Vietnam War, I nevertheless think that it is by reading the fiction—an act that takes time, reflection, and empathetic involvement with the human beings who move about in our minds as we feel what the fictional characters experience—that the essential truth of the Vietnam War can best be understood.

Journalist-turned-novelist, Japanese Takeshi Kaiko best sums up the tragedy in *Into a Black Sun*: "Perhaps Asian revolution was a banyan tree that tamed the men who sought to tame it, wore them out in endless conflict with a greedy incubus that left them wishing they were stone themselves. A tree that even then fed on its victims and sent out tentacles to snare and suck in more . . . and kill" (p. 143). Only when all conflicts such as occurred in Vietnam no longer exist, I'm afraid, will we be able to disprove this and the other sad truths we can discover by reading the fiction written about the Vietnam War.

Author/Title List
for the Bibliographic Commentary

Selected Bibliography
of the Interpretative Critique

Fiction

Anderson, Maxwell, and Laurence Stallings (1927). "What Price Glory." In *Three American Plays*. New York: Harcourt, Brace.

Baber, Asa (1970). *The Land of a Million Elephants*. London: Hutchinson.

Balaban, John (1982). *Blue Mountain*. Greensboro, N.C.: Unicorn Press. *POETRY*

Buck, Pearl S. (1931). *The Good Earth*. New York: John Day.

Bunting, Josiah (1972). *The Lionheads*. New York: George Braziller.

Burdick, Eugene, and William J. Lederer (1958). *The Ugly American* (New York: W. W. Norton).

Butler, Robert Olen (1981). *The Alleys of Eden*. New York: Horizon Press.

Camus, Albert (1954). Translated by Stuart Gilbert. *The Stranger*. New York: Vintage Books.

Collingwood, Charles (1970). *The Defector*. New York: Harper and Row.

Conrad, Joseph ([1902] 1973). *Heart of Darkness*. Harmondsworth, Eng.: Penguin Books.

Crane, Stephen ([1895] 1983). *The Red Badge of Courage*. New York: Penguin Books.

Del Vecchio, John (1982). *The 13th Valley*. New York: Bantam Books.

Eastlake, William (1969). *The Bamboo Bed*. New York: Simon and Schuster.

Ehrhart, William (1983). *Vietnam—Perkasie: A Combat Marine Memoir*. Jefferson, N.C.: McFarland.

Forster, E. M. (1924). *A Passage to India*. New York: Harcourt, Brace.

Fuller, Jack (1984). *Fragments*. New York: William Morrow.

Greenberg, Martin H., and Augustus Richard Norton (1985). *Touring Nam: The Vietnam War Reader*. New York: William Morrow.

Greene, Graham (1955). *The Quiet American*. Harmondsworth, Eng.: Penguin Books.

Groom, Winston (1978). *Better Times Than These*. New York: Berkley.

Halberstam, David (1968). *One Very Hot Day*. Boston: Houghton Mifflin.

Hemingway, Ernest (1929). *A Farewell to Arms*. New York: Charles Scribner's Sons.

Hobart, Alice (1933). *Oils for the Lamps of China*. Indianapolis, Ind.: Bobbs Merrill.

Homer (1984). *The Iliad*. Translated by Robert Fitzgerald. Oxford: Oxford University Press.

——— (1946). *The Odyssey*. Translated by E. V. Rieu. Harmondsworth, Eng.: Penguin Books.

Kalb, Bernard, and Marvin Kalb (1981). *The Last Ambassador*. Boston: Little, Brown.

Koestler, Arthur (1941). *Darkness at Noon*. New York: Macmillan.

Lawrence, D. H. ([1923] 1980). *Kangaroo*. Harmondsworth, Eng.: Penguin Books.

Little, Loyd (1978). *In the Village of the Man*. New York: Viking Press.

——— (1975). *Parthian Shot*. New York: Viking Press.

McCarry, Charles (1983). *The Last Supper*. New York: E. P. Dutton.

——— (1975). *The Tears of Autumn*. New York: E. P. Dutton.

McQuinn, Donald E. (1980). *Targets*. New York: Tom Doherty Associates.

Mailer, Norman (1948). *The Naked and the Dead*. New York: Holt, Rinehart and Winston.

Miller, Arthur ([1953] 1976). *The Crucible*. New York: Penguin Books.

Nguyen, Du (1973). *The Tale of Kieu*. Translated by Huynh Sanh Thong. New York: Vintage Books.

O'Brien, Tim (1978). *Going After Cacciato*. New York: Delacorte Press.

Pratt, John Clark (1974). *The Laotian Fragments*. New York: Avon Books.

———, comp. (1984). *Vietnam Voices: Perspectives on the War Years, 1941–1982*. New York: Viking Penguin.

Pelfrey, William (1972). *The Big V*. New York: Liveright.

Remarque, Erich M. (1929). *All Quiet on the Western Front*. Boston: Little, Brown.

Stone, Robert (1973). *Dog Soldiers*. Boston: Houghton Mifflin.

Webb, James (1978). *Fields of Fire*. Englewood Cliffs, N.J.: Prentice-Hall.

——— (1981). *A Sense of Honor*. New York: Bantam Books.

Weigl, Bruce (1985). *The Monkey Wars*. Athens: University of Georgia Press.

West, Morris (1965). *The Ambassador*. New York: William Morrow.

Weston, Christine G. (1943). *Indigo*. New York: Charles Scribner's Sons.

Wilson, Sloan (1955). *The Man in the Gray Flannel Suit*. New York: Simon and Schuster.

Winn, David (1982). *Gangland*. New York: Alfred A. Knopf.

Wright, Stephen (1983). *Meditations in Green*. New York: Charles Scribner's Sons.

Nonfiction

Andrews, William R. (1973). *The Village War: Vietnamese Communist Revolutionary Activities in Dinh Tuong Province, 1960–1964*. Columbia: University of Missouri Press.

Basham, A. L. (1959). *The Wonder That Was India*. New York: The Grove Press.

Beidler, Philip D. (1982). *American Literature and the Experience of Vietnam*. Athens: University of Georgia Press.

Benedict, Ruth (1946). *The Chrysanthemum and the Sword: Patterns of Japanese Culture*. Boston: Houghton Mifflin.

Borton, Lady (1984). *Sensing the Enemy: An American Woman Among the Boat People of Vietnam*. New York: Doubleday.

Broyles, William, Jr. (1985). "A Veteran's Return to Vietnam: The Road to Hill 10." *Atlantic Monthly* (April): 90–118.

Bryan, C. D. B. (1984). "Barely Suppressed Screams: Getting a Bead on Vietnam War Literature." *Harper's* (June): 67–72.

——— (1976). *Friendly Fire*. New York: G. P. Putnam's Sons.

Buttinger, Joseph (1968). *Vietnam: A Political History*. New York: Frederick A. Praeger.

Caputo, Philip (1977). *A Rumor of War*. New York: Ballantine Books.

Cleaver, Eldridge (1968). *Soul on Ice*. New York: McGraw-Hill.

Colbert, Evelyn (1977). *Southeast Asia in International Politics, 1941–1956*. Ithaca, N.Y.: Cornell University Press.

Cox, Elizabeth (1984). "Veni, Vidi, and Then What: Walker Percy on 'Homo Loquens' and His Pilgrimage in the Modern Age." Honor's thesis, Middlebury College.

Dawson, Alan (1977). *55 Days: The Fall of South Vietnam*. Englewood Cliffs, N.J.: Prentice-Hall.

Devillers, Philippe, and Jean Lacouture (1969). *End of a War: Indochina, 1954*. New York: Frederick A. Praeger.

Downs, Frederick (1978). *The Killing Zone: My Life in the Vietnam War*. New York: W. W. Norton.

Duiker, William J. (1982). *The Communist Road to Power in Vietnam*. Boulder, Colo.: Westview Press.

Ellsberg, Daniel (1972). *Papers on the War*. New York: Simon and Schuster.

Emerson, Gloria (1976). *Winners and Losers*. New York: Random House.

Fairbank, John K. (1983). *The United States and China*. Fourth, enlarged edition. Cambridge, Mass: Harvard University Press.

Fall, Bernard B. (1956). *The Viet-Minh Regime*. New York: Institute of Pacific Relations.

Fanon, Frantz (1963). *The Wretched of the Earth*. Translated by Constance Farrington. New York: Grove Press.

Fifield, Russell H. (1963). *Southeast Asia in United States Policy*. New York: Frederick A. Praeger.

FitzGerald, Frances (1972). *Fire in the Lake: The Vietnamese and the Americans in Vietnam*. New York: Random House.

Fromkin, David and James Chace (1985). "The Lessons of Vietnam?" *Foreign Affairs* 63: 722–46.

Fussell, Paul (1975). *The Great War in Modern Memory*. New York: Oxford University Press Galaxy Books.

Gaddis, John Lewis (1982). *Strategies of Containment: A Critical Appraisal of Postwar American National Security Policy*. Oxford: Oxford University Press.

Gates, John M. (1973). *Schoolbooks and Krags: The U.S. Army in the Philippines*. Westport, Conn.: Greenwood Press.

Gelb, Leslie H., with Richard K. Betts (1979). *The Irony of Vietnam: The System Worked*. Washington, D.C.: Brookings Institution.

Halberstam, David (1972). *The Best and the Brightest*. New York: Random House.

Harrison, James P. (1982). *The Endless War: Fifty Years of Struggle in Vietnam*. New York: Free Press.

Herr, Michael (1978). *Dispatches*. New York: Alfred A. Knopf.

Holsti, Ole R., and James N. Rosenau (1984). *American Leadership in World Affairs: Vietnam and the Breakdown of Consensus*. Boston: Allen and Unwin.

Iriye, Akira (1974). *The Cold War in Asia: A Historical Introduction*. Englewood Cliffs, N.J.: Prentice-Hall.

Isaacs, Arnold R. (1983). *Without Honor: Defeat in Vietnam and Cambodia*. Baltimore: Johns Hopkins University Press.

Kennan, George F. (1984). *American Diplomacy*. Expanded edition. Chicago: University of Chicago Press.

Kierkegaard, Søren (1980). *Sickness Unto Death*. Translated by Howard V. Hong and Edna H. Hong. Princeton, N.J.: Princeton University Press.

Klein, Joe (1985). *Payback*. New York: Ballantine Books.

Kovic, Ron (1976). *Born on the Fourth of July*. New York: McGraw-Hill.

Le Thanh Khoi (1955). *Le Viet-Nam: Histoire et Civilisation*. Paris: Editions de Minuit.

Levenson, Joseph R. (1964). *Confucian China and Its Modern Fate* 2 vols. Berkeley: University of California Press.

Lewy, Guenter (1978). *America in Vietnam*. New York: Oxford University Press.

Lin Yutang (1944). *The Wisdom of China and India*. New York: Random House.

Littauer, Raphael, and Norman Uphoff, eds. (1972). *The Air War in Indochina*. Revised edition. Boston: Beacon Press.

Lomperis, Timothy J. (1984). *The War Everyone Lost—and Won: America's Intervention in Vietnam's Twin Struggles*. Baton Rouge: Louisiana State University Press.

Luce, Don, and John Sommer (1969). *Viet Nam—The Unheard Voices*. Ithaca, N.Y.: Cornell University Press.

McGarvey, Patrick J., ed. (1969). *Visions of Victory: Selected Vietnamese Communist Military Writings, 1964–1968*. Stanford, Calif.: Hoover Institution on War, Revolution and Peace.

MacPherson, Myra (1985). *Long Time Passing: Vietnam and the Haunted Generation*. New York: Doubleday.

Manchester, William (1980). *Goodbye Darkness: A Memoir of the Pacific War*. New York: Dell.

Marr, David G. (1971). *Vietnamese Anticolonialism, 1885–1925*. Berkeley: University of California Press.

Mus, Paul (1952). *Viet Nam: Sociologie d'une Guerre*. Paris: L'Editions du Seuil.

Newman, John (1982). *Vietnam War Literature*. Metuchen, N.J.: Scarecrow Press.

Oberdorfer, Don (1971). *Tet!* New York: Doubleday.

Percy, Walker (1975). *Message in a Bottle*. New York: Farrar, Straus and Giroux.

Pike, Douglas (1966). *Vietcong: The Organization and Techniques of the National Liberation Front of South Vietnam*. Cambridge, Mass.: MIT Press.

Plato (1941). *Republic*. Translated by Francis MacDonald Cornford. London: Oxford University Press.

Popkin, Samuel L. (1979). *The Rational Peasant: The Political Economy of Rural Society in Vietnam*. Berkeley: University of California Press.

Pratt, John Clark, comp. (1984). *Vietnam Voices: Perspectives on the War Years, 1941–1982*. New York: Viking Penguin.

Race, Jeffrey (1972). *War Comes to Long An: Revolutionary Conflict in a Vietnamese Province*. Berkeley: University of California Press.

Reischauer, Edwin O. (1977). *The Japanese*. Cambridge, Mass.: Harvard University Press.

Salisbury, Harrison E. (1967). *Behind the Lines—Hanoi*. New York: Harper and R ..

Santoli, Al (1985). *To Bear Any Burden: The Vietnam War and Its Aftermath in the Words of Americans and Southeast Asians*. New York: E. P. Dutton.

———— (1981). *Everything We Had: An Oral History of the Vietnam War by Thirty-three American Soldiers Who Fought it*. New York: Random House.

Sheehan, Neil, et. al. (1971). *The Pentagon Papers—As Published by the* New York Times. New York: Bantam Books.

Snepp, Frank (1977). *Decent Interval*. New York: Random House.

Spear, Percival (1972). *India: A Modern History*. Revised edition. Ann Arbor: University of Michigan Press.

Terry, Wallace (1984). *Bloods*. New York: Random House.

Thompson, Virginia (1937). *French Indo-China*. New York: Macmillan.

Thomson, James C., Jr., Peter W. Stanley, and John Curtiss Perry (1981). *Sentimental Imperialists: The American Experience in East Asia*. New York: Harper and Row.

Truong Buu Lam (1967). "Patterns of Vietnamese Response to Foreign Intervention: 1858–1900." *Southeast Asia Studies* 11: 1–151.

Truong Nhu Tang, with David Chanoff and Doan Van Toai (1985). *A Vietcong Memoir*. San Diego: Harcourt Brace Jovanovich.

Tuchman, Barbara (1984). *The March of Folly: From Troy to Vietnam*. New York: Alfred A. Knopf.

Van Tien Dung (1977). *Our Great Spring Victory: An Account of the Liberation of South Vietnam*. Translated by John Spragens, Jr. New York: Monthly Review Press.

West, Francis J., Jr. (1972). *The Village*. New York: Harper and Row.

Westmoreland, William C. (1976). *A Soldier Reports*. Garden City, N.Y.: Doubleday.

Woodside, Alexander B. (1976). *Community and Revolution in Modern Vietnam*. Booton: Houghton Mifflin.

List of Named Participants

Approximately seventy writers, educators, and publishers attended The Asia Society conference on 7–9 May 1985. The following is an abridged list of participants who are referred to in the foregoing interpretative critique. The majority of the participants listed are either Vietnam veterans or had experience in Vietnam during the war. Reference is made below to their relevant writings and current activities.

Asa Baber is a contributing editor at *Playboy* magazine and the author of *The Land of a Million Elephants* (1970).

John Balaban, professor of English at Pennsylvania State University, poet and translator of Vietnamese folk poetry, is also the author of the novel *Coming Down Again* (1985).

Philip Beidler, professor of English and assistant dean of the graduate school at the University of Alabama, is the author of *American Literature and the Experience of Vietnam* (1982).

Lady Borton is the author of *Sensing the Enemy: An American Woman Among the Boat People of Vietnam* (1984) and is working on a TV documentary about healing from the war.

William Broyles, a contributing editor to *U.S. News and World Report*, is the author of *Brothers in Arms: A Journey from War to Peace* (1986).

C. D. B. Bryan, a free-lance writer, is the author of the nonfiction account *Friendly Fire* (1976) among other writings.

Robert Olen Butler teaches creative writing at McNeese State University, Lake Charles, Louisiana, and is the author of *On Distant Ground* (1985), *Alleys of Eden* (1981), and *Wabash* (1987).

James Chace, editor, public affairs, for the *New York Times Book Review*, is the author of *Endless War: How We Got Involved in Central America . . . and What Can be Done* (1984) and "What *Are* the Lessons of Vietnam?" (*Foreign Affairs*, 1985).

Frederick Downs, director, prosthetic and sensory aids service of the Veterans Administration, is the author of *The Killing Zone* (1978).

John Del Vecchio is the author of the novel *The 13th Valley* (1982) among numerous reviews and articles.

Arthur Egendorf, psychologist, initiated a congressional study of the war's impact called "Legacies of Vietnam" and is the author of *Healing from the War: Trauma and Transformation After Vietnam* (1985).

William Ehrhart, writer, editor, and teacher, has published numerous volumes of poetry and prose and is most recently the editor of *Carrying the Darkness: American Indochina—the Poetry of the Vietnam War* (1985).

Joseph Ferrandino, a writer who has recently completed a new novel *Eleven Bravo*, was one of the designers of the New York Vietnam Veterans Memorial.

Lydia Fish, professor of anthropology, State University College at Buffalo, is involved with that university's Vietnam Veterans Oral History and Folklore Project.

Jack Fuller, editorial page editor, the *Chicago Tribune*, is the author of *Fragments* (1984). His most recent novel is *Mass* (1985).

James Harrison, professor of history at Hunter College in New York, is the author of *The Endless War: Fifty Years of Struggle in Vietnam* (1982).

Arnold Isaacs, author of *Without Honor: Defeat in Vietnam and Cambodia* (1983), is a journalist who was stationed in Saigon for the *Baltimore Sun*.

Juris Jurjevics was editor-in-chief at Dial Press for seven years and is now publisher of the Soho Press.

Joe Klein is the author of *Woody Guthrie: A Life* (1980) and *Payback: Five Marines After Vietnam* (1985). He contributes articles to *Esquire, New York,* and *Rolling Stone*.

Ron Kovic is the author of *Born on the Fourth of July* (1976) and *Around the World in Eight Days* (1985).

Lawrence Lichty, professor and chairman, department of radio, TV, and film at Northwestern University, was director of research for the WGBH series "Vietnam: A Television History."

Timothy J. Lomperis, assistant professor of political science, Duke University, is the author of *Vietnam: The War Everyone Lost—and Won: America's Intervention in Vietnam's Twin Struggles* (1984).

Myra MacPherson, a writer for the *Washington Post*, is the author of *Long Time Passing: Vietnam and the Haunted Generation* (1985).

Tim O'Brien, a writer, is the author of *Going After Cacciato* (1978), *If I Die in a Combat Zone* (1973), and *The Nuclear Age* (1985).

Robert Oxnam, president of The Asia Society, is the author of *Ruling From Horseback* (1975) among other publications on contemporary Asian affairs.

Abe Peck, director of magazine studies and assistant professor, The Medill School of Journalism, Northwestern University, is the author of *Uncovering the 60's: The Life and Times of the Underground Press* (1985).

William Pelfrey, author of *The Big V* (1972), has published many articles on South and Southeast Asia in leading journals.

John Clark Pratt, professor of English at Colorado State University, is author of the novel *The Laotian Fragments* (1974) and compiled *Vietnam Voices: Perspectives on the War Years, 1941–1982* (1984).

Colonel John W. Ripley is the senior Marine Corps representative at the United States Naval Academy and the director of English and history there.

Al Santoli, contributing editor, *Parade*, is the author of *Everything We Had* (1978) and *To Bear Any Burden* (1985).

Michael Stephens, a writer, is the author of *The Dramaturgy of Style* (1986) and the play *Horse*.

Wallace Terry, journalist and author of *Bloods: An Oral History of the Vietnam War by Black Veterans* (1984), recently wrote and produced the 1986 TV documentary "The Bloods of 'Nam."

James Webb, currently assistant secretary of defense (reserve affairs), is the author of *Fields of Fire* (1978), *A Sense of Honor* (1981), and *A Country Such As This* (1983).

Bruce Weigl, professor of English at Pennsylvania State University, has published a volume of poetry, *The Monkey Wars* (1985).

John Wheeler, president of the Project on the Vietnam Generation at the Smithsonian Institution, is the author of *Touched with Fire: The Future of the Vietnam Generation* (1984).

David Winn, a professor of English at Hunter College in New York, is the author of the novel *Gangland* (1982).

Stephen Wright, a novelist, is the author of *Meditations in Green* (1983).

Conference Program

The Vietnam Experience in American Literature, 7–9 May 1985, The Asia Society

Tuesday Evening, 7 May

OPENING ADDRESS

Welcoming remarks by Robert B. Oxnam, President, The Asia Society
Opening address by James Webb, Assistant Secretary of Defense and author of *Fields of Fire*

Wednesday, 8 May

LITERATURE ON THE WAR EXPERIENCE

Combat Literature
Moderator: Lawrence Lichty, University of Maryland
Panelists: John Del Vecchio (*The 13th Valley*), Jack Fuller (*Fragments*), William Pelfrey (*The Big V*)

Fact and Fiction in the Literature
Moderator: Michael Stephens, Columbia University
Panelists: Tim O'Brien (*Going After Cacciato*), Wallace Terry (*Bloods*), Bruce Weigl (*The Monkey Wars*), Stephen Wright (*Meditations in Green*)

LITERATURE ON THE WAR'S IMPACT
ON A GENERATION OF AMERICANS

Literature on the Veteran Experience
Moderator: Joseph Ferrandino, Columbia University
Panelists: William Ehrhart (*Vietnam—Perkasie*), Joe Klein (*Payback*), Ron Kovic (*Born on the Fourth of July*)

The Impact on Those at Home
Moderator: Abe Peck, Northwestern University
Panelists: C. D. B. Bryan (*Friendly Fire*), Myra MacPherson (*Long Time Passing: Vietnam and the Haunted Generation*), David Winn (*Gangland*)

Thursday, 9 May

Images of Asia and Asians in the Literature
Moderator: Timothy Lomperis, Duke University
Panelists: Asa Baber (*The Land of a Million Elephants*), John Balaban (*Blue Mountain*), Al Santoli (*To Bear Any Burden*)

The Role of Literature in Understanding the War
Moderator: Robert B. Oxnam, The Asia Society
Panelists: Philip Beidler (*American Literature and the Experience of Vietnam*), James Chace, *New York Times*, John Clark Pratt (*Vietnam Voices*)

Index to Interpretative Critique

Library of Congress Cataloging-in-Publication Data
Lomperis, Timothy J., 1947–
"Reading the wind."
"Published for The Asia Society."
Bibliography: p.
Includes index.
1. American literature—20th century—History and
criticism. 2. Vietnamese Conflict, 1961–1975—Literature
and the war. 3. Vietnamese Conflict, 1961–1975—Personal
narratives, American. 4. War stories, American—History
and criticism. 5. American literature—20th century—
Bibliography. 6. Vietnamese Conflict, 1961–1975—
Biography. I. Pratt, John Clark. II. Asia Society.
III. Title. IV. Series.
PS228.V5L66 1987 810'.9'358 86-23982
ISBN 0-8223-0705-7
ISBN 0-8223-0749-9 (pbk.)